**DATE DUE**

| NOV 9 '77 | | | |
|---|---|---|---|
| | | | |
| | | | |
| | | | |
| | | | |
| | | | |
| | | | |
| | | | |
| | | | |
| | | | |
| | | | |

**Political Leadership in America**

SCOTT FORESMAN PROBLEMS IN AMERICAN HISTORY

*General Editors:* **Edwin Fenton,** *Carnegie-Mellon University*
**David H. Fowler,** *Carnegie-Mellon University*

*Volumes in this series:*

**THE CAUSES OF WAR:**
The American Revolution, The Civil War, and World War 1
*Kenyon C. Cramer*

**THE NEGRO IN AMERICA**
*Larry Cuban*

**LABOR IN AMERICAN SOCIETY**
*Raymond S. Iman and Thomas W. Koch*

**THE SUPREME COURT IN AMERICAN LIFE**
*Leonard F. James*

**AMERICAN FOREIGN POLICY**
*Leonard F. James*

**THE SOCIAL SETTING OF INTOLERANCE:**
The Know-Nothings, The Red Scare, and McCarthyism
*Seymour J. Mandelbaum*

**REFORM IN AMERICA:**
Jacksonian Democracy, Progressivism, and The New Deal
*Faye Rattner*

**GREAT DEPRESSIONS:**
1837–1844, 1893–1898, 1929–1939
*John Sperling*

**POLITICAL LEADERSHIP IN AMERICA**
*Emmett Wright, Jr.*

# Political Leadership in America

**Emmett Wright, Jr.,** *Instructor in American History*
*Westminster Boys School, Atlanta*

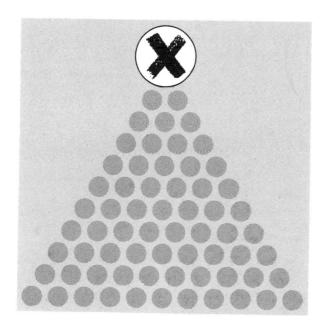

**SCOTT, FORESMAN AND COMPANY**

COVER DESIGN BY ED BEDNO

# Editors' Introduction

Growing numbers of history teachers realize that using source materials in their courses provides an added dimension of experience for their students. Total reliance on a textbook can no longer be considered an adequate means of learning history. Yet if the full value of documents and critical articles is to be obtained, they must be presented as something more than writings which record important events or as mere illustrations of what the text says. They must also challenge the student's ability to relate individual events to larger topics and to continuing themes in history.

Each volume of the Scott Foresman Problems in American History organizes source materials around one facet of our nation's past. A volume contains fifteen Problems, each designed for one day's work. In some of the books the Problems are intended to be read individually, at the proper chronological intervals. In others, they are grouped into three units of five Problems each, such a unit being best used as an uninterrupted week's work. Whether the Problems are studied individually or in units, they should be assigned only after the student has read the relevant material in his textbook.

One of the most vital services a collection of source materials can perform is to encourage the student to develop his critical abilities to the utmost in constructing historical explanations. Interpretation is the heart of history; the student should be brought to realize how essential it is to be able to do more with facts than memorize them. The SCOTT FORESMAN PROBLEMS are specifically designed to engage the student in the fascinating task of interpreting American history. Through them he will gain the skills and the enjoyment which come from reaching insight and understanding as well as knowledge of history.

Each Problem begins with an introduction written by the author to place documents in their historical context and to link together the Problems in a volume. These introductions prepare the student to read intelligently by defining the scope of the Problem, suggesting its relationship to larger issues, and pointing out difficulties of interpretation so that he will not attempt the impossible in generalizing from limited evidence.

The study questions at the end of the introduction carry the student further in applying the historian's critical tools. He may be asked to try to judge the reliability of a document or the bias of a critic, to assess an historical interpretation in the light of his knowledge, or to reason from particulars to a general conclusion of his own. Properly used, the study questions help beginning students find out what is important in source materials; without them, students often do not know what they are supposed to do with the readings.

To obtain more from a Problem than simply answers to the author's questions, the student should first read the introduction and questions and then pause to review what he already knows about the subject. Then, keeping the central issues in mind, he should study the entire Problem, perhaps first skimming through it to see the relationship of the parts to the whole, and then reading it carefully and taking notes. He will then be ready to consider his answers to the study questions in preparation for class discussion.

The teacher can use the SCOTT FORESMAN PROBLEMS in several ways. A Problem can perhaps serve most effectively as the basis for discussion by an entire class, with the lesson organized around the study questions or other questions proposed by the teacher to develop new points of view. What seems most appropriate for discussion will always depend partly upon the textbook used in the course and partly upon the instructor's own style of teaching and command of the subject. Each teacher should structure the discussion around those issues which he thinks are most important, but he should take care to link a Problem to those which precede and which follow it. These connecting links give the student the maximum opportunity to comprehend the theme of the volume. By treating a limited number of issues within each Problem, a teacher should be able to restrict discussion to one class period.

These volumes can be used in other ways. Many readings can serve as the basis for reports to the class by individual students. An entire volume, or a selection of Problems from a volume, may be used in preparing a controlled research paper; the three-unit volumes are especially suited to this purpose. The Problems may also be assigned as supplementary reading in those areas where text treatment is not extensive.

In *Political Leadership,* Emmett Wright, Jr. examines the careers of fifteen prominent American leaders who performed different functions in politics and who used various methods to achieve their goals. The material that Wright has chosen describes the setting in which each man worked and the particular problems he faced. Wright's discussion of these men provides a framework which the student can use to gain insight into and an understanding of American political leadership.

EDWIN FENTON
DAVID H. FOWLER

8

# Table of Contents

# Author's Introduction

In any society some persons stand out as leaders. They may be leaders in any number of fields—business, religion, the arts, education, or politics. Whatever the field, leaders possess certain qualities that enable them to guide other persons. This book is about fifteen American political leaders. It examines each man's contributions to politics, the personal characteristics which equipped him to lead, and the political situation in which he led.

People usually think of political leaders as office holders in the executive, legislative, or judicial branches of national, state, or local governments. Men and women such as these have won sufficient respect to be elected or appointed to positions of power and trust which enable them to make decisions. The decisions they make as public officials affect the welfare and activities of many people.

Some of the fifteen men discussed in this volume were important primarily as decision makers, that is, as elected or appointed governmental officials. Others had their greatest influence outside the formal structure of government. Although some men in the latter group did, in fact, hold office, their posts were not essential to their greatest impact as political leaders. These leaders affected American society through the power of their personalites, their ability to pull strings behind the scenes, or their persuasive arguments. Political scientists call them *agitators, manipulators,* or *political theorists.*

An agitator seeks to bring about change by arousing public discussion and demanding action on some particular issue. He may hold office, but often does not. A manipulator differs from an agitator. While the latter appeals to the public, the former prefers to work behind the scenes. Usually the manipulator operates within the framework of a political party (as a big city boss, for example), and he often holds a public office as well. A theorist examines political facts and events and tries to influence his fellow citizens toward a particular course of action by the way in which he explains or analyzes them. Whether or not he holds public office is relatively unimportant to his major political role.

Leaders differ also in goals. Some have fought to preserve the old order against the attacks of reformers. Others have worked to overthrow the established order. Still others have attempted to change the political and social system by revision—keeping some parts of the old and replacing others. Finally, some men have devoted their energies to create a new order once the old one had been destroyed, just as the delegates to the Constitutional Convention strove to develop a new central government in the 1780's.

A potential political leader must have resources to influence people. His personality, native intelligence, education, wealth, social standing, and identification with his followers in religious belief or ethnic background may help. The particular resources he requires depend upon time and circumstance.

Personal resources alone are not enough. Whether a man can utilize his resources to lead depends largely upon his political skills. Some men have been gifted at the art of compromise. They obtained parts of their programs by giving way on some matters which seemed to be not so essential. Others were perceptive enough to change with the times; they altered specific proposals to reach the general goals of their programs. Still other leaders—even in the face of changing circumstances—clung stubbornly to both their long range goals and their specific programs. Although such stubbornness sometimes had disastrous results, men like these often attracted a host of followers who admired their defiant dedication to principle. Obviously, differing circumstances call for different sets of political skills.

When a man seeks political leadership, his life is often changed. But, in turn, he may change the society of which he is a part. Because politics touches all of our lives and dominates the careers of so many great Americans, it is a fascinating study.

EMMETT WRIGHT, JR.

PROBLEM **1**

# John Winthrop:
# Man with a Mission

American history abounds with accounts of leaders inspired by visions of a new society. Men who felt a sense of mission planted colonies along the Atlantic coast, explored and settled the West, built cities and towns, and developed industries. They inspired other persons to follow their vision.

A leader with a sense of mission has a number of advantages as well as some handicaps. Belief in his cause sustains him amid great troubles. The early leaders of the Mormons, mid-nineteenth century converts to a new religion, were supported by a strong sense of mission. They led their persecuted followers from New York through Illinois to find sanctuary on the shores of the Great Salt Lake.

A sense of mission can also handicap a leader. Convinced that his cause is just and right, he may refuse to listen to his opponents or consider the possibility that he could be wrong. In a democratic society where the ability to compromise is the essence of politics, a leader with a mission often fails because he cannot adjust to the realities of political life. Yet without such leaders the colonies might never have been successful. The first settlers of Massachusetts accepted the leadership of

William Bradford and John Winthrop because of their infectious and fervent belief in their undertaking.

John Winthrop, the first governor of the Massachusetts Bay Colony, sought to establish and maintain a Puritan theocracy. In 1634 the freemen of the colony accused Winthrop and other leaders of not allowing them a part in making laws. When he failed to convince voters that the restrictions on voting were defensible, he temporarily lost influence in the colony. However, this belief in his own infallibility helped found and sustain the colony through its most difficult years.

The two excerpts in Problem 1 reveal aspects of Winthrop's character which reflect his abilities as a leader. As you read them, keep the following questions in mind:

**1**     What were Winthrop's outstanding character traits? What was his philosophy of government? How did these traits and philosophy of government suit him for political leadership?

**2**     What was Winthrop's conception of the relationship between the voter and elected officials? What was the basis of this belief?

**3**     Could a man of Winthrop's character succeed in contemporary American politics? Why?

# I

## THE SETTING AND THE MAN

Edmund S. Morgan, professor of American history at Yale gives vivid insights into the problems faced by John Winthrop in establishing a government under Puritan leadership.  □  Edmund S. Morgan, *The Puritan Dilemma: The Story of John Winthrop,* pp. 84–95. Boston: Little, Brown and Company. Copyright © 1958 by Edmund S. Morgan. Reprinted by permission of the author and Little, Brown and Company.

When Winthrop and eleven other members of the Massachusetts Bay Company met at Cambridge, England, on August 26, 1629, they agreed to go to New England if the charter and headquarters of the company could be transferred with them. Ten of the twelve kept their pledge, eight of them arriving with Winthrop or shortly after. Besides these, Winthrop could count only four or five other members of the company in New England at the end of 1630. This handful of men was now the Massachusetts Bay Company and endowed with all the powers described in the charter which Winthrop guarded among his papers.

In the charter the King had granted authority "to make, ordeine, and establishe all manner of wholesome and reasonable orders, lawes, statutes, and ordinances, directions, and instructions, not contrarie to the lawes of this our realm of England, as well for setling of the forms and ceremonies of government and magistracy fitt and necessary for the said plantation, and the inhabitants there, and for nameing and stiling of all sortes of officers, both superior and inferior, which they shall finde needeful for that governement and plantation, and the distinguishing and setting forth of the severall duties, powers, and lymytts of every such office and place." . . .

With regard to the organization and government of the company itself the charter was much more specific. The members, known as "freemen," were to meet four times a year in a "Great and General Court," to make laws for both company and colony. Once a year, at one of these courts, they would elect a governor, a deputy governor, and eighteen "assistants" for the coming year, to manage affairs between meetings of the General Court. This executive council was to meet every month. The governor or deputy governor and at least six of the assistants must be present also at every meeting of the General Court, but the charter did not specify that any other members must be present to constitute a quorum, so that these seven officers, in the absence of any other members, could presumably exercise all the powers of the General Court.

In Massachusetts, therefore, Winthrop and the dozen or so members of the company who came with him had unlimited authority to exercise any kind of government they chose over the other settlers. In order to satisfy the terms of the charter they had only to meet once a month as assistants (all but one of the members who are known to have migrated the first year were assistants) and four times a year as a General Court, though the two types of meeting would now be virtually indistinguishable in membership. Provided they followed this procedure and passed no laws repugnant to the laws of England, they could govern Massachusetts in any way they saw fit. And for that matter, who was to say what law was repugnant to those of England? Who was to decide, who to correct them if they erred? Here was no King, Parliament, bishop, or judge to stand in their way.

A group of men as sure of their cause as were Winthrop and his friends must have been strongly tempted to establish themselves as a permanent aristocracy or oligarchy, holding fast the power granted in the charter and using it to enforce the special commission which they believed God had given them. They were a determined, stiff-jawed set, quick to anger and slow to laughter, as likely a group of oligarchs as ever assembled. . . .

These . . . men, all disposed in their different ways to command those around them, were equipped also with a philosophy of government to give their commands a superhuman sanction. For more than a hundred years Protestants had been confronting the pope with declarations of the God-given authority of civil rulers. In England Anglican and Puritan alike maintained the divine right of their king against the enemy at Rome, who claimed a power to depose Protestant monarchs. Though the Puritans reserved to the people a right of resistance against tyrants who violated the laws of God, they were always ready to quote the Epistle to the Romans in support of rulers who enforced the laws of God. And the members of the Massachusetts Bay Company were all godly men; they had come with no other intention than to see God's will done at last.

Winthrop never lost an opportunity to affirm his belief that the powers that be were ordained of God and must be honored and respected accordingly. While still aboard the *Arbella* [the ship that brought him to America], he had reminded the other passengers that "God Almightie in his most holy and wise providence hath soe disposed of the Condicion of mankinde, as in all times some must be rich some poore, some highe and eminent in power and dignitie; others meane and in subjeccion." There was no doubt in Winthrop's mind that God intended civil governments to be in the hands of men like himself; [that] to entrust the people at large with powers of government, as in a Greek democracy, was not only unwarranted by Scripture but dangerous to the peace and well-being of the community, for the people at large were unfit to rule. The best part of them was always the smallest part, "and of that best part the wiser part is always the lesser."

Winthrop and the other members of the Bay Company were authorized by their charter to exercise absolute powers of government; they were endowed by temperament with the inclination to exercise those powers; and they were assisted by a philosophy of government which clothed every civil ruler in the armor of divine authority. How natural, then, that they should become a ruling oligarchy. They might readily have succumbed to the lust for power, since power lay unchallenged in their hands.

But they did not succumb. They did not even keep the powers to which the charter entitled them.

After Winthrop had explored the bay and moved the headquarters of the colony from Salem to Charlestown, he summoned the assistants for their first meeting on August 23, 1630. There were seven members present besides himself and [Thomas] Dudley [deputy governor], and they got down to the business of government at once. They provided for the maintenance of two ministers, set maximum wages for workmen in various trades, and appointed a beadle "to attend upon the Governor, and alwaies to be ready to execute his commands in publique businesses." They also ordered that there should be regular meetings, or "courts," of the assistants and of the General Court, though the difference between the two would be a formality, since their membership would be virtually identical (unless future emigration brought over other company members without the status of assistant). On September 7 and September 28 they met again as assistants and exercised their authority in a variety of actions. They forbade the sale of firearms to the Indians; they put an embargo on corn; they seized Richard Clough's strong water because he sold too much of it to other men's servants; and they fined Sir Richard Saltonstall, one of their own number, for being absent from Court.

Then on October 19 Winthrop summoned at Charlestown the first meeting labeled in the records as a General Court. For this day he and the seven company members who met with him had prepared a revolution that was to affect the history of Massachusetts from that time forward. The records described the event with tantalizing brevity: "For the establishinge of the government. It was propounded if it were not the best course that the Freemen should have the power of chuseing Assistants when there are to be chosen, and the Assistants from amongst themselves to chuse a Governor and Deputy Governor, whoe with the Assistants should have the power of makeing lawes and chuseing officers to execute the same."

This was surely a strange proposal to make to a group of men all of whom were both freemen and assistants. Why, when there were no freemen but themselves in the colony, should they make provision for freemen electing the assistants and the assistants electing the other officers? One begins to get an inkling of what was happening in the next sentence of the records: "This was fully assented unto by the generall vote of the people, and ereccion of hands."

The "people" here referred to were not simply the eight company members present. This we can conclude from events that followed. Winthrop had apparently thrown open the first meeting of the General Court to the whole body of settlers assembled at Charlestown. Together they had established the first constitution of Massachusetts. It used the terminology of the charter, and presumably allowed the provisions of the charter not expressly revised to remain in effect. But by general vote of the people of Massachusetts, the assistants were transformed from an executive council into a legislative assembly; and the term "freeman" was transformed from a designation for the members of a commercial company, exercising legislative and judicial control over that company and its property, into a designation for the citizens of a state, with the right to vote and hold office. The right of the citizen freemen to vote, however, was confined to electing assistants. These assistants, and not the freemen themselves, were to make laws and appoint from their own number a governor and deputy governor.

This transformation of the Bay Company's charter into a constitution for government of the colony would scarcely have been necessary or desirable if the members of the company had intended to keep control in their own hands. The reduction of the freemen's role in the government and the securing of popular consent to this change presaged the admission to freemanship of a large proportion of settlers, men who could contribute to the joint stock nothing but godliness and good citizenship. The transformation of trading company into commonwealth was completed at the next meeting of the General Court, when one hundred and sixteen persons were admitted as freemen. (This was probably most, if not all, of the adult males, excluding servants, then in the colony.) The new freemen then voted that elections should be annual and, doubtless at the behest of Winthrop, that "for time to come noe man shalbe admitted to the freedome of this body politicke, but such as are members of some of the churches within the lymitts of the same." Though stated in the form of a limitation, this declaration was in fact an open invitation to every future church member in Massachusetts to take up the privileges of freemanship.

Since the people had no political rights under the charter, Winthrop had given them a role to which they had had no legal claim at all. That he confined the gift to church members was not surprising: he would scarcely have wished to take into partnership all of the multitude of men who might come to his colony for the wrong reasons, and the qualified franchise might also help attract the right kind of settlers. By limiting freemanship to church members he extended political rights to a larger proportion of the people than enjoyed such rights in England—and to people who were better qualified to use them than the mere possessors of a forty-shilling freehold. The question that needs to be answered is not why he limited suffrage but why he extended it. What induced Winthrop and the other members of the Bay Company to resign voluntarily the exclusive powers which the charter conferred on them and which their political beliefs and native dispositions made congenial?

Possibly they gave way to popular demand, but there is no evidence that any such demand existed. Possibly they felt a need to keep their own ranks filled. With sickness and death whittling away at their number, they were already close to the minimum quota of seven assistants required by the charter for the holding of the Assistants Court (only six were required in the General Court). But granting their need to perpetuate themselves, they could still have filled vacancies with a few hand-picked men as the need arose. The charter gave them express permission to admit new members to the company if they chose, but it put them under no obligation to do so. Even a popular demand, if it existed, could have been met by a less drastic measure than the one they took.

The real answer as to why they opened the door to freemanship so wide is to be found in the terms of the commission with which they believed the colony was entrusted. The idea of a "covenant," or contract, between God and man occupied a pre-eminent place in their thought: it was the basis of an individual's salvation; it was the origin of every true church and also of every state. "It is of the nature and essence of every society," Winthrop once wrote, "to be knitt together by some Covenant, either expressed or implyed." God's special commission to Massachusetts was an implied covenant.

But there was more than one covenant involved in the establish ment of any society. After the people joined in covenant with God, agreeing to be bound by his laws, they must establish a government to see those laws enforced, for they did not have enough virtue to carry out their agreement without the compulsive force of government. They must decide among themselves what form of government they wanted and then create it by a voluntary joint compact—a second covenant.

Winthrop evidently thought that the mere act of coming to Massachusetts constituted a sufficient acceptance of the basic covenant, the special commission which God had given the colony. But the second covenant, establishing the government, required a more explicit agreement. Though the King's charter gave the Bay Company a clear and exclusive right to govern the territory, the King's authority was insufficient. The "due form of government" which Winthrop believed the special commission called for could originate only from a covenant between the settlers and the men who were to rule them. Hence the extraordinary action of October 19, with its sequel, the extension of freemanship.

Winthrop did not believe that in extending freemanship he had transformed Massachusetts into a democracy. The legislative power was lodged not in the people but in a select group where, according to his reading of the Bible, it belonged. Nor was Winthrop's action in securing the consent of the people to his government an affirmation of the principle that governments derive their just powers from the consent of the governed. He did not believe that the officers chosen under the new system would be simply the agents of the people who elected them. Rulers, however selected, received their authority from God, not from the people, and were accountable to God, not to the people. Their business was to enforce the nation's covenant with God, and during their term of office, so long as they devoted themselves to this business, they were free to act as they thought best, suiting their actions to the circumstances.

Winthrop did believe that the people, or a properly qualified portion of them, were entitled to determine the form of government to be established over them and to select the persons who should run that government. These two operations performed, their role was played out until, under the form of government they had chosen, it was time to elect new rulers. If a ruler failed in his duty to enforce the laws of God, the people would be obliged to turn him out without waiting for election time. But so long as he did his duty, his authority was absolute, and, regardless of any errors of judgment he might make, the people were obliged to submit. Indeed, anything less than submission would be rebellion against the authority of God.

In Winthrop's view, then, he had not in any way limited or reduced the authority of government by extending to church members a voice in the selection of the men who were to exercise the authority. Rather he had given to government a practical strength which it could not otherwise have possessed, for Winthrop was enough of a politician to know that, regardless of any divine authority a ruler might claim, people would submit to him more readily if they had a voice in choosing him, especially a Puritan people well educated by their ministers in the principle of government based on covenant.

There was a danger, of course, that the people would choose the wrong kind of men to rule them. Government was a difficult business, not something that one honest man could do as well as another. It required not only virtue but learning and wisdom as well: learning because the laws of God were not so obvious that he who runs might read them, wisdom because the ruler must be able to apply the laws every day to new situations and choose the right law for the case in hand. But the limitation of freemanship to church members furnished some insurance against the wiles of demagogues. Winthrop counted on the ministers to give the people sound advice and to instruct them about the kind of men who were best fitted to rule.

# II

## JOHN WINTHROP ON THE NATURE OF GOVERNMENT

In 1645, while John Winthrop was serving as deputy governor of Massachusetts Bay Colony, he was impeached on the ground that he had exceeded his authority. After three months of controversy, he was acquitted. On that occasion he delivered the speech which follows. It has become a classic statement of Puritan political thought.  ☐  James Kendall Hosmer, *Winthrop's Journal, 1630–1649,* Volume 2, p. 238. New York: Charles Scribner's Sons, copyright © 1908.

The great questions that have troubled the country, are about the authority of the magistrates and the liberty of the people. It is yourselves who have called us to this office, and being called by you, we have our authority from God, in way of an ordinance, such as hath the image of God eminently stamped upon it, the contempt and violation whereof hath been vindicated with examples of divine vengeance. I entreat you to consider, that when you choose magistrates, you take them from among yourselves, men subject to like passions as you are. Therefore when you see infirmities in us, you should reflect upon your own, and that would make you bear the more with us, and not be severe censurers of the failings of your magistrates, when you have continual experience of the like infirmities in yourselves and others. We account him a good servant, who breaks not his covenant. The covenant between you and us is the oath you have taken of us, which is to this purpose, that we shall govern you and judge your causes by the rules of God's laws and our own, according to our best skill. When you agree with a workman to build you a ship or house, etc., he undertakes as well for his skill as for his faithfulness, for it is his profession, and you pay him for both. But when you call one to be a magistrate, he doth not profess nor undertake to have sufficient skill for that office, nor can you furnish him with gifts, etc., therefore you must run the hazard of his skill and ability. But if he fail in faithfulness, which by his oath he is bound unto, that he must answer for. If it fall out that the case be clear to common apprehension, and the rule clear also, if he transgress here, the error is not in the skill, but in the evil of the will: it must be required of him. But if the case be doubtful, or the rule doubtful, to men of such understanding and parts as your magistrates are, if your magistrates should err here, yourselves must bear it.

PROBLEM 2

# Samuel Adams: Master of Propaganda

Agitators have played key roles throughout history. In America Samuel Adams and Patrick Henry rallied the colonists to revolt against England. During the mid-nineteenth century, Northern abolitionists and fire-eating Southern radicals helped drive in the wedge that eventually split the South from the North.

People in all parts of the world have responded to the appeal of agitators. This kind of political leader has blossomed in every free society, leading hundreds of movements with widely different goals. Because agitators desire change—and in a hurry—few have been conservative. Many have tried to turn the political clock back to an earlier day, and more have tried to create a new order or to revise the current one.

Agitators usually have pictured themselves as virtuous men striving for an ideal. Although historians can cite numerous exceptions, many agitators have been selfless, driving themselves mercilessly, even risking their lives. Many of them have died in relative obscurity, honored only by a remnant of the crowd which once cheered them.

Samuel Adams serves to introduce the role of the agitator in American politics. More than any other man, he kept the revolutionary flame burning through the late 1760's and early 1770's when others were willing to let it flicker and die. Born in Boston in 1722 and graduated from Harvard in 1740, Adams showed an early aptitude for politics. After working briefly as a merchant's clerk, he resigned to spend more of his time in politics, which had become his passion. Throughout the 1760's and 1770's, he devoted himself to speaking and writing about the conflict between the American colonies and England. Problem 2 presents excerpts from these writings and estimates of Adams' impact on the American Revolution.

As you read, think about the following questions:

**1** What were Adams' goals? How did he hope to achieve them?

**2** What personal characteristics made Adams a leader? What were his outstanding political skills?

**3** Would his characteristics and skills have fitted Adams to work in a formal political structure?

**4** How does the evaluation of Adams by Mercy Warren contrast with that by Hutchinson? How do these opinions help you assess Adams as a leader?

# I

## ADAMS DENOUNCES THE STAMP

The Stamp Act was greeted in the colonies with the general feeling that Parliament had overextended its authority when it levied a direct tax on a people not directly represented in that body. In a speech before the Assembly, Samuel Adams, a newly elected member, discussed the issue and addressed certain remarks especially to the Royal Governor of Massachusetts, Thomas Hutchinson. The following reading is taken from his speech. □ William V. Wells, *The Life and Public Services of Samuel Adams,* Volume 1, pp. 72–74. Boston: Little, Brown, and Company, copyright © 1865.

Your Excellency tells us that the Province seems to be upon the brink of a precipice! A sight of its danger is then necessary for its preservation. To despair of the Commonwealth is a certain presage of its fall. Your Excellency may be assured that the representatives of the people are awake to a sense of its danger, and their utmost prudence will not be wanting to prevent its ruin.

Your Excellency is pleased to tell us that declarations have been made and still subsist, that the act of Parliament for granting the stamp duties in the Colonies shall not be executed within the Province. We know of no such declarations. If any individuals of the people have declared an unwillingness to subject themselves to the payment of the stamp duties, and choose rather to lay aside all business than to make use of the stamped papers, we are not accountable for such declarations, so neither can we see anything criminal in them. This House [of Representatives] has no authority to control their choice in this matter. The act does not oblige them to make use of the papers; it only exacts the payment of certain duties for such papers as they may incline to use. Such declarations may possibly have been made and may still subsist very consistently with the utmost respect to the King and Parliament. . . .

You are pleased to say that the Stamp Act is an act of Parliament, and as such ought to be observed. This House, sir, has too great a reverence for the supreme legislature of the nation to question its just authority. It by no means appertains to us to presume to adjust the boundaries of the power of Parliament; but boundaries there undoubtedly are. We hope we may, without offence, put your Excellency in mind of that most grievous sentence of excommunication solemnly denounced by the Church in the name of the sacred Trinity, in the presence of King Henry the Third and the estates of the realm, against all those who should make statutes or observe them being made contrary to the liberties of Magna Charta. We are ready to think those zealous advocates for the Constitution usually compared their acts of Parliament with Magna Charta; and if it ever happened that such acts were made as infringed upon the rights of that charter, they were always repealed. . . .

Furthermore, your Excellency tells us that the right of the Parliament to make laws for the American Colonies remains indisputable in Westminster. Without contending this point, we beg leave just to observe that the charter of this Province invests the General Assembly with the power of making laws for its internal government and taxation; and that this charter has never yet been forfeited. The Parliament has a right to make all laws within the limits of their own Constitution. Among these, is the right of representation in the same body which exercises the power of taxation. There is a necessity that the subjects of America should exercise this power within themselves, otherwise they can have no share in that most essential right, for they are not represented in Parliament, and indeed we think it impracticable. Your Excellency's assertion leads us to think that you are of a different mind with regard to this very material point, and that you suppose we are represented; but the sense of the nation itself seems always to have been otherwise. The right of the Colonies to make their own laws and tax themselves has been never, that we know of, questioned; but has been constantly recognized by the King and Parliament. The very supposition that the Parliament, though the supreme power over the subjects of Britain universally, should yet conceive of a despotic power within themselves, would be most disrespectful; and we leave it to your Excellency's consideration, whether to suppose an indisputable right in any government to tax the subjects without their consent, does not include the idea of such a power.

Our duty to the King, who holds the rights of all his subjects sacred as his own prerogative, and our love to our own constituents and concern for their dearest interests, constrain us to be explicit upon this very important occasion. We beg that your Excellency would consider the people of this Province as having the strongest affection for his Majesty, under whose happy government they have felt all the blessings of liberty: they have a warm sense of the honor, freedom, and independence of the subjects of a patriot king; they have a just value for those inestimable rights, which are derived to all men from nature, and are happily interwoven in the British Constitution; they esteem it sacrilege for them to ever give them up; and rather than lose them they would willingly part with everything else. We deeply regret it that the Parliament has seen fit to pass such an act as the Stamp Act. We flatter ourselves that the hardships of it will shortly appear to them in such a point of light as shall induce them in their wisdom to repeal it. In the mean time, we must beg your Excellency to excuse us from doing anything to assist in the execution of it.

# II

## A REPLY TO GOVERNOR HUTCHINSON

Parliamentary authority was a subject that engaged Samuel Adams' attention during most of his political career. His writings, speeches, and activities challenged the authority of the British Parliament over the colonial governments, particularly that of Massachusetts. By 1773 many Massachusetts towns had adopted the "Rights of the Colonists," a set of declarations (mainly the work of Adams) against Parliamentary supremacy; and Governor Thomas Hutchinson, in an effort to prevent further disloyalty, called a meeting of the Assembly. In a message to both houses of the Legislature, he called on the colonists to debate the issue of the supreme authority of Parliament. Samuel Adams welcomed the opportunity to answer the governor, and on January 26, 1773, he spoke before the House of Representatives. The following excerpt is from his speech. □ Harry Alonzo Cushing, Editor, *The Writings of Samuel Adams,* pp. 424–426. New York: G. P. Putnam's Sons, copyright © 1906.

Your Excellency tells us, "you know of no line that can be drawn between the supreme authority of Parliament and the total independence of the colonies." If there be no such line, the consequence is, either that the colonies are the vassals of the Parliament, or that they are totally independent. As it cannot be supposed to have been the intention of the parties in the compact, that we should be reduced to a state of vassalage, the conclusion is, that it was their sense, that we were thus independent. "It is impossible," your Excellency says, "that there should be two independent Legislatures in one and the same state." May we not then further conclude, that it was their sense, that the colonies were, by their charters, made distinct states from the mother country? Your Excellency adds, "for although there may be but one head, the King, yet the two Legislative bodies will make two governments as distinct as the kingdoms of England and Scotland, before the union." Very true, may it please your Excellency; and if they interfere not with each other, what hinders, but that being united in one head and common Sovereign, they may live happily in that connection, and mutually support and protect each other? Notwithstanding all the terrors which your Excellency has pictured to us as the effects of a total independence, there is more reason to dread the consequences of absolute uncontroled power, whether of a nation or a monarch, than those of a total independence. It would be a misfortune "to know by experience, the difference between the liberties of an English colonist and those of the Spanish, French, and Dutch": and since the British Parliament has passed an act, which is executed even with rigor, though not voluntarily submitted to, for raising a revenue, and appropriating the same, without the consent of the people who pay it, and have claimed a power of making such laws as they please, to order and govern us, your Excellency will excuse us in asking, whether you do not think we already experience too much of such a difference, and have not reason to fear we shall soon be reduced to a worse situation than that of the colonies of France, Spain, or Holland?

If your Excellency expects to have the line of distinction between the supreme authority of Parliament, and the total independence of the colonies drawn by us, we would say it would be an arduous undertaking, and of very great importance to all the other colonies; and therefore, could we conceive of such a line, we should be unwilling to propose it, without their consent in Congress.

To conclude, these are great and profound questions. It is the grief of this House, that, by the ill policy of a late injudicious administration, America has been driven into the contemplation of them. And we cannot but express our concern, that your Excellency, by your speech, has reduced us to the unhappy alternative, either of appearing by our silence to acquiesce in your Excellency's sentiments, or of thus freely discussing this point.

After all that we have said, we would be far from being understood to have in the least abated that just sense of allegiance which we owe to the King of Great Britain, our rightful Sovereign; and should the people of this province be left to the free and full exercise of all the liberties and immunities granted to them by charter there would be no danger of an independence on the Crown. Our charters reserve great power to the Crown in its Representative, fully sufficient to balance, analogous to the English constitution, all the liberties and privileges granted to the people. All this your Excellency knows full well; and whoever considers the power and influence, in all their branches, reserved by our charter, to the Crown will be far from thinking that the Commons of this province are too independent.

# III

## GOVERNOR HUTCHINSON ATTACKS ADAMS

Governor Hutchinson had long been one of Samuel Adams' favorite targets, and the governor did not underestimate the influence exercised by his vocal opponent. The following excerpt from a letter indicated how Hutchinson regarded Adams. □ James Kendall Hosmer, *The Life of Thomas Hutchinson*, pp. 215–216. Boston: Houghton, Mifflin and Company. Copyright © 1896 by James K. Hosmer.

I doubt whether there is a greater incendiary in the King's dominion or a man of greater malignity of heart, who less scruples any measure ever so criminal to accomplish his purposes; and I think I do him no injustice when I suppose he wishes the destruction of every friend to government in America. This is the man who is of the . . . [Committee of Correspondence] and the *instar omnium* [one who stands for, or is head of, all others] with which the agent [Benjamin Franklin] corresponds and from which he takes his directions in the recess of the [British] Court. The doctrine advanced in these letters of independence upon Parliament and even upon the King to whom they deny the right of supporting or even instructing his Governor, must rouse the people of England and they will sooner or later express their indignation. I see the principle spreading every day, and the silence in England is construed to be a tacit acknowledgment or acquiescence. It cannot, as they threaten, be expressly acknowledged, but it may, and as soon as we ... think ourselves strong enough, will be openly asserted and all attempts to secure our dependence openly resisted.

# IV

## AN ADMIRER PRAISES ADAMS

Samuel Adams had many enemies, but he had as many, if not more, admirers. Mrs. Mercy Warren, the sister of James Otis, shared her brother's enthusiasm for colonial independence and valued Adams' dedication to the cause. The brief excerpt below reflects her devotion to him. ☐ William V. Wells, *The Life and Public Services of Samuel Adams,* Volume 1, p. 411. Boston: Little, Brown, and Company, copyright © 1865.

Early nurtured in the principles of civil and religious liberty, he possessed a quick understanding, a cool head, stern manners, a smooth address, and a Roman-like firmness, united with that sagacity and penetration that would have made a figure in a conclave. He was at the same time liberal in opinion, and uniformly devout; social with men of all denominations; grave in deportment; placid, yet severe; sober and indefatigable; calm in seasons of difficulty; tranquil and unruffled in the vortex of political altercation; too firm to be intimidated, too haughty for condescension, his mind was replete with resources that dissipated fear, and extricated in the greatest emergencies. Thus qualified, he stood forth early, and continued firm through the great struggle, and may justly claim a large share of honor due to that spirit of energy which opposed the measures of administration, and produced the Independence of America. Through a long life he exhibited, on all occasions, an example of patriotism, religion, and virtue, honorary to the human character.

# V

## THE JUDGMENT OF A MODERN HISTORIAN

In his book, *The Epic of America,* historian James Truslow Adams discusses Samuel Adams' role as an agitator, or, as he phrases it, a manipulator of the masses. A twentieth-century American scholar, James Truslow Adams, examines Samuel Adams' personality as well as his political tactics. Portions of his work are reprinted in the reading which follows.  ☐  James Truslow Adams, *The Epic of America,* pp. 81–85. Boston: Atlantic—Little, Brown, and Company, copyright © 1931, 1933; copyright renewed 1959 by James Truslow Adams. Reprinted by permission.

[The] greatest master in manipulating the masses whom America has ever seen, except possibly Bryan, arose in Boston. Opinions will always differ regarding Samuel Adams, but there can be no difference of opinion as to his consummate ability as a plotter of revolution. In all else he was a failure throughout his life. Before the years in which his manipulation of the inflammable material among the public was to give him a lasting place in American history, he had failed in law and business and public office. In after years, when constructive work had to be done in Congress in constitution making or as governor of his new State, he played a wholly insignificant part. He could tear down, but not build up. He was a fanatic, as most men are who change history, and with a fanatical hatred of England he strove to break all ties with her. . . . Even when others had no wish to secede from the empire, but merely to be left in peace or to have certain inimical laws repealed, Adams early conceived the belief that the one end to work for was immediate and complete independence.

As he surveyed the field of public opinion in which he would have to operate, he saw clearly the two classes of rich and poor and realized that their interests were different. The rich were conservative, the poor radical; the rich were desirous of as little change as possible, the poor clamored for any change that would better their condition; the rich would be influenced mainly by arguments of compromise and expediency, the poor by appeals to their rights for a greater share in the political and economic life of their communities. If these two classes could be brought to work together, public opinion would be a unit, but if they could not, then the greater reliance must be placed on the poorer classes, who constituted the overwhelming mass of the population and who could more readily be stirred to anger and radical action. From about 1761 until independence was declared by the colonies in 1776, Adams worked ceaselessly for the cause to which he had devoted his life, manipulating newspapers and town meetings, organizing committees of correspondents throughout the colonies, even bringing about happenings which would inflame public opinion. At one period it looked as though his efforts would be in vain, but in the end the stupidity of the British government won the day for him.

It is a great mistake to think of public opinion as united in the colonies and as gradually rising against British tyranny. Public opinion is never wholly united, and seldom rises to a pitch of passion without being influenced—in other words, without the use of propaganda. . . .

From the first, Adams and those working with him had realized the necessity of democratic slogans in the creation of a state of mind. While the merchants were busy pointing out to their London correspondents that the new laws would hurt the business of all alike, Adams at once struck boldly out to inflame the passions of the crowd by threatening that it was to be reduced to the "miserable state of tributary slaves," contrasting its freedom and moral virtue with the tyranny and moral degradation of England. He proclaimed that the mother country was bent on bringing her colonies to a condition of "slavery, poverty and misery," and on causing their utter ruin, and dinned into the ears of the people the words "slavery and tyranny" until they assumed a reality from mere reiteration. His political philosophy was eagerly lapped up by a populace smarting under hard times and resentful of colonial even more than imperial conditions of the moment. The establishment of government by free consent of all had become imbedded in the mind of the average man, as an essential part of the American dream. Adams himself had seen the vision, but had glimpsed it with the narrowness and bitterness with which the more bigoted Puritans had seen the vision of an unloving and revengeful Hebrew Jehovah. Like them he felt that he alone, and those who believed as he did, were in possession of the truth, and that those who differed from him were enemies of truth and God. Because, however, the American dream had so deeply affected the hopes and aspirations of the common men, the more radical among them, in town and on frontier, echoed with wild enthusiasm such pronouncements of Adams as that "the natural liberty of man is to be free from any superior power on earth, and not to be under the will or legislative authority of man, but only to have the law of nature for his rule."

Such talk as this could only make England fearful of how far the people might try to put such precepts into practice. The upper classes in the colonies also began to be uneasy. Up to 1770, when their own grievances were redressed, they might allow such ideas to be disseminated, considering themselves in control of the situation, but after that it became clear that they were losing control. Whereas such men as John Hancock and John Adams wanted quiet, and retired from public affairs to the management of their own, Sam Adams and the lesser radicals worked harder than ever to keep public opinion inflamed.

With the upper classes become lukewarm or hostile to his continued propaganda, with the obnoxious legislation repealed or modified, he had to trust to generalizations and emotional appeals. A good example of his use of the latter was the affair called the "Boston Massacre." As part of the general imperial policy following the war, the British government had stationed some regiments in Boston. They were under good officers and good discipline, and there was no more reason why they should have made trouble there than in any provincial garrison town of England. Adams, however, was continually stirring up the public mind against them; John Adams reported finding him one Sunday night "preparing for the next day's newspaper—a curious employment, cooking up paragraphs, articles, occurrences, etc., working the political engine." Finally, one March evening, as a result of more than usual provocation given by taunting boys to soldiers on duty, an unfortunate clash occurred. There was confusion, a rioter's shout to "fire" was mistaken for an officer's command, and several citizens were killed. The officer surrendered to the civil authorities, was tried, defended by John Adams and Josiah Quincy, Jr., and acquitted. But Samuel Adams at once saw the value of the incident. Every emotion of the mob was played upon. The affair was termed a "massacre," and in the annual speeches given for a number of years to commemorate its anniversary the boys and men who had taken part in the mobbing were described as martyrs to liberty and the soldiers as "bloody butchers." Although there is no recorded instance of a soldier having offered the slightest affront to any Boston girl, orators ranted about "our beauteous virgins exposed to all the insolence of unbridled passion—our virtuous wives, endeared to us by every tender tie, falling a sacrifice to worse than brutal violence and perhaps, like the famed Lucretia, distracted with anguish and despair, ending their wretched lives by their own fair hands." At the request of the citizens the troops were removed from the city, but such talk, which served its intended purpose, was kept up for years after. The incident was unimportant in itself, and its chief interest is in how the radicals, after having provoked it, made use of it.

PROBLEM 3

# Alexander Hamilton:
# Theorist as Politician

Alexander Hamilton was a theorist. He represents the type of leader who influences his followers through his analyses and explanations of political facts and events. Hamilton's greatest contributions to American politics were made through his ideas on government and government policy and through the force of his mind.

As a delegate to a convention held at Annapolis in 1786, he became one of the leaders of a movement to frame a federal constitution that would replace the inadequate Articles of Confederation. The next year the Federal Constitutional Convention was held in Philadelphia for the purpose of writing a new constitution; Hamilton was a delegate from New York. He urged a strong centralized government, modeled on that of England, with an executive officer and senators chosen for life. Even though the delegates rejected many of his ideas, Hamilton later worked hard for the ratification of the Constitution that the delegates had framed in Philadelphia.

The ideas which Alexander Hamilton expressed on government continue to be controversial. Although generally accepted by conservatives, they are still a target for liberals, who attack Hamilton's belief in a government that would encourage industries and aid merchants and landowners. Hamilton was convinced that government could work only through "a representative democracy, where the right of election is well secured and regulated, and the exercise of the legislative, executive, and judiciary is vested in select persons."

Born sometime between 1755 and 1757 in the British West Indies, Hamilton was left to shift for himself at age eleven when his mother died. His burning ambition for a college education led him to New York and to Kings College in 1773. The following year found him engrossed in revolutionary activity. Hamilton's anonymous pamphlets attracted wide attention because of their grasp of the issues which were straining the relationship between the colonies and the mother country. His professors could not believe that a seventeen-year-old boy could produce such work. His writing was that of a moderate who, though defending the sovereignty of the crown, questioned the assumption of authority by Parliament.

As words led to action and the military phase of the Revolution came rushing on, Hamilton contributed his talents—first as commander of an artillery company, then as secretary and aide to General Washington. In this latter post a close relationship between the two men developed and led to Hamilton's prominence in Washington's administration. As Secretary of the Treasury in Washington's cabinet, Hamilton established a program that strengthened the nation economically and politically. During the next administration his advice was continually sought by members of Adams' cabinet.

The three readings in Problem 3 reflect Hamilton's philosophy, desires, and ability to compromise in regard to the new government under the Constitution.

As you read, keep the following questions in mind:

**1**    What was Hamilton's role in the writing and adoption of the Constitution? How had he been prepared through earlier experiences to accept that role?

**2**    What sort of government did Hamilton want? What sort did he accept? What political abilities must a theorist have if he wishes to have long-run influence?

**3**    How do the political skills of a successful theorist differ from those of a successful agitator?

**4**    Abraham Lincoln believed in "government of the people, by the people, and for the people." How would Hamilton have regarded Lincoln's well-known phrase?

# I

## "A MODEL GOVERNMENT"

Henry Cabot Lodge was accepted as a man of literary merit before he became
a United States Senator in 1893. Prior to that time he had published many
books, among them a biography of Alexander Hamilton and a nine-volume
collection of his works. In the excerpt which follows, the author comments
on Hamilton as a theorist, analyzing his concept of the ideal constitutional
government. Lodge also examines Hamilton as a politician, evaluating his
role as a supporter of the work of the Federal Constitutional Convention.
□ Henry Cabot Lodge, *Alexander Hamilton*, Volume 1, pp. 59–62. Boston:
Houghton Mifflin & Co., copyright © 1898.

In the course of his argument he [Hamilton] read his own plan for
the new government, carefully worked out and perfected. This plan,
which discloses the essence of his opinions on government, followed
in a general way the English system, as did all others presented, including
the one finally adopted.... But it embodied two ideas which were its
cardinal features, and which went to the very heart of the whole matter.
The republic of Hamilton was to be an aristocratic as distinguished from
a democratic republic, and the power of the separate States was to be
effectually crippled. The first object was attained by committing the
choice of the President and senators, who were to hold office during
good behavior, to a class of the community qualified to vote by the possession of a certain amount of real property. The second was secured
by giving to the President of the United States the appointment of the
governors of the various States, who were to have a veto on all state
legislation. These provisions, as may be seen at a glance, involved the
essential character of the government, and although purely republican,
came much nearer to the British model than any other by their recognition
of classes and of the political rights of property, while by the treatment
of the States a highly centralized national government was to supersede
entirely the confederate form. In the Congress of the Confederation,
Hamilton had seen that all the difficulties arose from the too great power
of the States, and further, as he believed, from the democratic form of
their governments. With his usual bold decision, therefore, he struck at
the root of the evils and struck hard. Many of the states-rights men in
the convention dreaded too much democracy, when applied to the people
of the United States collectively, but they were far from approving the
vigorous ideas of Hamilton. The majority of the members undoubtedly

favored a democratic system in the Union, such as they were familiar with in their own States. Even those who believed with Hamilton, that in the best government there should be an infusion of aristocracy, had no disposition to risk what was then deemed the last chance for a respectable union, on a scheme which would be hopeless of acceptance. There can be no doubt that Hamilton, with his keen perception of existing facts, was perfectly aware that the leading principles of his plan stood no chance of adoption, either by the people or the convention. The aim of his great speech and of his draft of a constitution was to brace the minds of his fellow members and to stimulate them to taking higher ground than the majority of their constituents demanded. In this he succeeded. His eloquent reasoning, if it did not lead men to his own conclusions, at least raised their tone, enlightened many members, and brought them to a more advanced ground than they were at first prepared to take. This was all of great importance, and to work for such results was, in Hamilton's isolated position, his wisest course.

His message once delivered, he waited and watched, aiding quietly and effectively whenever he could, but not attempting to thrust himself forward, fettered as he was by the action of his own State. His colleagues, however, abandoned the convention, and at the close Hamilton, not shrinking from the responsibility of representing alone a State where opinions adverse to his own prevailed, once more took part in the debates and affixed his name and that of New York to the Constitution. When the end was thus finally reached, he sprang once more to the front and gave free rein to all his activity and zeal. It was in this last decisive struggle, in securing the acceptance of the work of the convention, that Hamilton rendered his greatest services to the cause of the Constitution, —services more important and more effective than those of any other one man at this last stage of what was in truth a great political revolution.

# II

## HAMILTON'S IMPRESSIONS OF THE NEW GOVERNMENT

When the convention at Philadelphia completed its work in 1787, Hamilton noted his impressions of the Constitution. Whether intended as a letter to a friend, a memorandum for Hamilton's personal use, or a contribution for the newspapers, the following selection estimates the success of the new government. □ Henry Cabot Lodge, Editor, *The Works of Alexander Hamilton*, Volume 1, pp. 420–424. New York: G. P. Putnam's Sons, copyright © 1903.

The new Constitution has in favor of its success these circumstances: A very great weight of influence of the persons who framed it, particularly in the universal popularity of General Washington. The good-will of the commercial interest throughout the States, which will give all its efforts to the establishment of a government capable of regulating, protecting, and extending the commerce of the Union. The good-will of most men of property in the several States, who wish a government of the Union able to protect them against domestic violence, and the depredations which the democratic spirit is apt to make on property, and who are besides anxious for the respectability of the nation. The hopes of the creditors of the United States, that a general government possessing the means of doing it, will pay the debt of the Union. A strong belief in the people at large of the insufficiency of the present Confederation to preserve the existence of the Union, and of the necessity of the Union to their safety and prosperity; of course, a strong desire of a change, and a predisposition to receive well the propositions of the convention.

Against its success is to be put the dissent of two of three important men in the convention, who will think their characters pledged to defeat the plan; the influence of many *inconsiderable* men in possession of considerable offices under the State governments, who will fear a diminution of their consequence, power, and emolument, by the establishment of the general government, and who can hope for nothing there; the influence of some *considerable* men in office, possessed of talents and popularity, who, partly from the same motives, and partly from a desire of *playing a part* in a convulsion for their own aggrandizement, will oppose the quiet adoption of the new government (some considerable men out of office, from motives of ambition, may be disposed to act the same part). Add to these causes the disinclination of the people to taxes, and of course to a strong government; the opposition of all men much in debt, who will not wish to see a government established, one object of which is to restrain the means of cheating creditors; the democratical jealousy of the people, which may be alarmed at the appearance of institutions that may seem calculated to place the power of the community in few hands, and to raise a few individuals to stations of great pre-eminence; and the influence of some foreign powers, who . . . will not wish to see an energetic government established throughout the States.

In this view of the subject it is difficult to form any judgment whether the plan will be adopted or rejected. It must be essentially matter of conjecture. The present appearances and all other circumstances considered, the probability seems to be on the side of its adoption.

But the causes operating against its adoption are powerful, and there will be nothing astonishing in the contrary.

If... [the Constitution does not succeed in passage], it is probable the discussion of the question will beget such struggles, animosities, and heats in the community, that this circumstance, conspiring with the *real necessity* of an essential change in our present situation, will produce civil war. Should this happen, whatever parties prevail, it is probable governments very different from the present in their principles will be established. A dismemberment of the Union, and monarchies in different portions of it, may be expected. It may, however, happen that no civil war will take place, but several republican confederacies be established between different combinations of the particular States.

A reunion with Great Britain, from universal disgust at a state of commotion, is not impossible, though not much to be feared. The most plausible shape of such a business would be the establishment of a son of the present monarch in the supreme government of this country, with a family compact.

If the government be adopted it is probable General Washington will be the President of the United States. This will ensure a wise choice of men to administer the government, and a good administration. A good administration will conciliate the confidence and affection of the people, and perhaps enable the government to acquire more consistency than the proposed constitution seems to promise for so great a country. It may then triumph altogether over the State governments, and reduce them to an entire subordination, dividing the larger States into smaller districts. The *organs* of the general government may also acquire additional strength.

If this should not be the case in the course of a few years, it is probable that the contests about the boundaries of power between the particular governments and the general government, and the *momentum* of the larger States in such contests, will produce a dissolution of the Union. This, after all, seems to be the most likely result.

# III

## A DEFENSE OF THE CONSTITUTION

Hamilton's stirring defense of the Constitution in the New York convention clearly indicated his support of the new government. The failure of his state to ratify the Constitution would have cut the nation in two and denied the United States the wealth and strength which New York could bring. Hamilton's speeches on June 20 and 21, 1788, encouraged the New York ratifying convention to adopt the Constitution. ☐ Albert Bushnell Hart, Editor, *American History Told by Contemporaries*, Volume 3, pp. 242–246. New York: The Macmillan Company, copyright © 1902.

In order that the committee may understand clearly the principles on which the general Convention acted, I think it necessary to explain some preliminary circumstances. Sir, the natural situation of this country seems to divide its interests into different classes. There are navigating and non-navigating states. The Northern are properly navigating states: the Southern appear to possess neither the means nor the spirit of navigation. This difference of situation naturally produces a dissimilarity of interests and views respecting foreign commerce. It was the interest of the Northern States that there should be no restraints on their navigation, and they should have full power, by a majority in Congress, to make commercial regulations in favor of their own, and in restraint of the navigation of foreigners. The Southern States wish[ed] to impose a restraint on the Northern, by requiring that two thirds in Congress should be requisite to pass an act in regulation of commerce. They were apprehensive that the restraints of a navigation law would discourage foreigners, and, by obliging them to employ the shipping of the Northern States, would probably enhance their freight. This being the case, they insisted strenuously on having this provision ingrafted in the Constitution; and the Northern States were as anxious in opposing it. On the other hand, the small states, seeing themselves embraced by the Confederation upon equal terms, wished to retain the advantages which they already possessed. The large states, on the contrary, thought it improper that Rhode Island and Delaware should enjoy an equal suffrage with themselves. From these sources a delicate and difficult contest arose. It became necessary, therefore, to compromise, or the Convention must have dissolved without effecting any thing. Would it have been wise and prudent in that body, in this critical situation, to have deserted their country? No. Every man who hears me, every wise man in the United States, would have condemned them. The Convention were obliged to appoint a committee for accommodation. In this committee, the arrangement was formed as it now stands, and their report was accepted. It was a delicate point, and it was necessary that all parties should be indulged. Gentlemen will see that, if there had not been a unanimity, nothing could have been done; for the Convention had no power to establish, but only to recommend, a government. Any other system would have been impracticable. Let a convention be called to-morrow; let them meet twenty times,—nay, twenty thousand times; they will have the same difficulties to encounter, the same clashing interests to reconcile. . . .

. . . Sir, we hear constantly a great deal which is rather calculated to awake our passions, and create prejudices, than to conduct us to the truth, and teach us our real interests. I do not suppose this to be the design of the gentlemen. Why, then, are we told so often of an aristocracy? For my part, I hardly know the meaning of this word, as it is applied. If all we hear be true, this government is really a very bad one. But who are the aristocracy among us? Where do we find men elevated to a perpetual rank above their fellow-citizens, and possessing powers entirely independent of them? The arguments of the gentlemen only go to prove that there are men who are rich, men who are poor, some who are wise, and others who are not; that, indeed, every distinguished man is an aristocrat. This reminds me of a description of the aristocrats I have seen in a late publication styled the Federal Farmer. The author reckons in the aristocracy all governors of states, members of Congress, chief magistrates, and all officers of the militia. This description, I presume to say, is ridiculous. The image is a phantom. Does the new government render a rich man more eligible than a poor one? No. It requires no such qualification. It is bottomed on the broad and equal principle of your state constitution.

Sir, if the people have it in their option to elect their most meritorious men, is this to be considered as an objection? Shall the Constitution oppose their wishes, and abridge their most invaluable privilege? While property continues to be pretty equally divided, and a considerable share of information pervades the community, the tendency of the people's suffrages will be to elevate merit even from obscurity. As riches increase and accumulate in few hands, as luxury prevails in society, virtue will be in a greater degree considered as only a graceful appendage of wealth, and the tendency of things will be to depart from the republican standard. This is the real disposition of human nature: it is what neither the honorable member nor myself can correct; it is a common misfortune, that awaits our state constitution as well as all others. . . .

It is a harsh doctrine that men grow wicked in proportion as they improve and enlighten their minds. Experience has by no means justified us in the supposition that there is more virtue in one class of men than in another. Look through the rich and the poor of the community, the learned and the ignorant. Where does virtue predominate? The difference indeed consists, not in the quantity, but kind, of vices which are incident to various classes; and here the advantage of character belongs to the wealthy. Their vices are probably more favorable to the prosperity of the state than those of the indigent, and partake less of moral depravity.

After all, sir, we must submit to this idea, that the true principle of a republic is, that the people should choose whom they please to govern them. Representation is imperfect in proportion as the current of popular favor is checked. This great source of free government, popular election, should be perfectly pure, and the most unbounded liberty allowed. Where this principle is adhered to; where, in the organization of the government, the legislative, executive, and judicial branches are rendered distinct; where, again, the legislature is divided into separate houses, and the operations of each are controlled by various checks and balances, and, above all, by the vigilance and weight of the state governments,—to talk of tyranny, and the subversion of our liberties, is to speak the language of enthusiasm. This balance between the national and state governments ought to be dwelt on with peculiar attention, as it is of the utmost importance. It forms a double security to the people. If one encroaches on their rights, they will find a powerful protection in the other. Indeed, they will both be prevented from overpassing their constitutional limits, by a certain rivalship, which will ever subsist between them. I am persuaded that a firm union is as necessary to perpetuate our liberties as it is to make us respectable; and experience will probably prove that the national government will be as natural a guardian of our freedom as the state legislature[s] themselves.

Suggestions, sir, of an extraordinary nature, have been frequently thrown out in the course of the present political controversy. It gives me pain to dwell on topics of this kind, and I wish they might be dismissed. We have been told that the old Confederation has proved inefficacious, only because intriguing and powerful men, aiming at a revolution, have been forever instigating the people, and rendering them disaffected with it. This, sir, is a false insinuation. The thing is impossible. I will venture to assert, that no combination of designing men under heaven will be capable of making a government unpopular which is in its principles a wise and good one, and vigorous in its operations.

The Confederation was framed amidst the agitation and tumults of society. It was composed of unsound materials, put together in haste. Men of intelligence discovered the feebleness of the structure, in the first stages of its existence; but the great body of the people, too much engrossed with their distresses to contemplate any but the immediate causes of them, were ignorant of the defects of their constitution. But when the dangers of war were removed, they saw clearly what they had suffered, and what they had yet to suffer, from a feeble form of government. There was no need of discerning men to convince the people of their unhappy situation; the complaint was coëxtensive with the evil, and both were common to all classes of the community. We have been told that the spirit of patriotism and love of liberty are almost extinguished among the people, and that it has become a prevailing doctrine that republican principles ought to be hooted out of the world. Sir, I am confident that such remarks as these are rather occasioned by the heat of argument than by a cool conviction of their truth and justice. As far as my experience has extended, I have heard no such doctrine; nor have I discovered any diminution of regard for those rights and liberties, in defence of which the people have fought and suffered. There have been, undoubtedly, some men who have had speculative doubts on the subject of government; but the principles of republicanism are founded on too firm a basis to be shaken by a few speculative and skeptical reasoners. Our error has been of a very different kind. We have erred through excess of caution, and a zeal false and impracticable. Our counsels have been destitute of consistency and stability. I am flattered with the hope, sir, that we have now found a cure for the evils under which we have so long labored. I trust that the proposed Constitution affords a genuine specimen of representative and republican government, and that it will answer, in an eminent degree, all the beneficial purposes of society.

PROBLEM 4

# John C. Calhoun:
# Theorist of the Lost Cause

Most political theorists are not active political leaders. Many are on the fringe of politics, holding offices which have no great influence. Active politicians for the most part are practical men who face the demands of office every day. Because they must be informed about public opinion, they must stay in touch with their constituents by talking or corresponding with them. They must also keep informed on the technical aspects of issues confronting government. Therefore, they spend much of their time conferring with colleagues and experts who are qualified to advise them. The demands of public office make it difficult for a man to take time in the middle of a busy political career to write political philosophy.

John C. Calhoun was both an active politician and a political theorist. His family were pioneers who had become prosperous enough in the South Carolina uplands to own a few slaves. Self-taught until he reached age eighteen, Calhoun then attended a preparatory school for two years before entering Yale College as a junior. In 1807 he was admitted to the South Carolina bar. Although his legal practice in Abbeville was successful, Calhoun did not enjoy it. In his first attempt to win public office in 1808 he was elected to the state legislature. Two years later he was elected to the United States House of Representatives. His public life was to span almost a half-century of American political ferment.

A modern American historian, Richard Hofstadter, described Calhoun as a brilliant, if narrow, logician and "the last American statesman to do any primary political thinking." What kind of personality brought this brilliant mind to the systematic development of political theory? Contemporaries saw in Calhoun a man obsessed with the discharge of duty. Indeed, Calhoun once wrote: "I hold the duties of life to be greater than life itself." Essentially a serious man, he found great solace in long periods of solitary reflection.

As a member of Congress, Calhoun held a position of power and prestige. He served as acting chairman and then as chairman of the House Committee on Foreign Relations. While much evidence supports the thesis that Calhoun began his public career an ardent nationalist, remaining in that camp even when writing for states' rights, sectional considerations eventually came to be his one major cause.

The gradual but mounting opposition in the North to Negro slavery found Calhoun among the first to defend the South and its "peculiar institution." He was the first nationally known Southern political leader to declare in Congress that slavery was a "positive good." By the mid-1840's Calhoun became concerned about Northern efforts, through control of Congress, to monopolize new territories and thereby prohibit slavery in those territories. In the end Calhoun's search for a privileged position for the South in the Union failed, and civil war followed.

In the readings for Problem 4, Calhoun is shown at three stages of his career. In the first reading he appears as a young Congressman speaking in favor of war against England. In the second reading he writes as the Vice President, explaining his principle of nullification. In the third reading he speaks, at the age of sixty-eight, as a dying statesman defending his beloved South. As you read, keep the following questions in mind:

1    How did Calhoun support his pro-war position in 1811? Is his justification for war enough to label him as a nationalist? Did he seem to be speaking for any particular section of the country?

2    Was Calhoun a nationalist or a sectionalist in 1832? How did he support his position?

3    What was his position on nationalism and sectionalism in 1850? How did he support it?

4    What would you say was Calhoun's major function as a political leader in the South during the period from 1811 to 1850?

# I

## A WAR HAWK SPEAKS OF WAR

In 1811, as relations between the United States and Great Britain worsened, a young member of the House Committee on Foreign Relations, John C. Calhoun, spoke for the committee in favor of a bill to increase the size of the army. The following excerpt from Calhoun's speech is his reply to Congressman John Randolph, who had disputed the recommendations of the committee and had pointed out a number of dangers that the United States, still a young and weak country, would face by passing legislation which could lead to war. ☐ Richard K. Crallé, Editor, *Speeches of John C. Calhoun*, Volume 2, pp. 1–3. New York: D. Appleton and Company, copyright © 1853.

I understood the opinion of the Committee on Foreign Relations, differently from what the gentleman from Virginia (Mr. Randolph) has stated to be his impression. I certainly understand that the committee recommended the measures now before the House, as a preparation for war; and such, in fact, was its express resolve, agreed to, I believe, by every member, except that gentleman. I do not attribute any wilful misstatement to him, but consider it the effect of inadvertency or mistake. Indeed, the Report [of the Committee on Foreign Relations] could mean nothing but war or empty menace. I hope no member of this House is in favor of the latter. A bullying, menacing system, has every thing to condemn and nothing to recommend it. In expense, it almost rivals war. It excites contempt abroad, and destroys confidence at home. Menaces are serious things; and ought to be resorted to with as much caution and seriousness, as war itself; and should, if not successful, be invariably followed by it. . . . The resolve contemplates an additional regular force; a measure confessedly improper but as a preparation for war, but undoubtedly necessary in that event.

Sir, I am not insensible to the weighty importance of the proposition, for the first time submitted to this House, to compel a redress of our long list of complaints against one of the belligerents. According to my mode of thinking, the more serious the question, the stronger and more unalterable ought to be our convictions before we give it our support. War, in our country, ought never to be resorted to but when it is clearly justifiable and necessary; so much so, as not to require the aid of logic to convince our understandings, nor the ardor of eloquence to inflame our passions. There are many reasons why this country should never resort to war but for causes the most urgent and necessary. It is sufficient that, under a government like ours, none but such will justify it in the eyes of the people; and were I not satisfied that such is the present case, I certainly would be no advocate of the proposition now before the House.

Sir, I might prove the war, should it ensue, justifiable, by the express admission of the gentleman from Virginia;—and necessary, by facts undoubted, and universally admitted; such as he did not pretend to controvert. The extent, duration, and character of the injuries received; the failure of those peaceful means heretofore resorted to for the redress of our wrongs, are my proofs that it is necessary. Why should I mention the impressment of our seamen; depredations on every branch of our commerce, including the direct export trade, continued for years, and made under laws which professedly undertake to regulate our trade with other nations; negotiation resorted to, again and again, till it is become hopeless; the restrictive system persisted in to avoid war, and in the vain expectation of returning justice? The evil still grows, and, in each succeeding year, swells in extent and pretension beyond the preceding. The question, even in the opinion and by the admission of our opponents is reduced to this single point—Which shall we do, abandon or defend our own commercial and maritime rights, and the personal liberties of our citizens employed in exercising them? These rights are vitally attacked, and war is the only means of redress. The gentleman from Virginia has suggested none, unless we consider the whole of his speech as recommending patient and resigned submission as the best remedy. Sir, which alternative this House will embrace, it is not for me to say. I hope the decision is made already, by a higher authority than the voice of any man. It is not for the human tongue to instil the sense of independence and honor. This is the work of nature; a generous nature that disdains tame submission to wrongs.

# II

## CALHOUN WRITES OF NULLIFICATION

At the second stage in his career, Calhoun was faced with a dilemma. The Tariff of 1828 was unpopular in South Carolina because it protected new industries in the Northeast at the expense of the entire nation. Calhoun realized that by supporting the economic interests of his state he would lose favor with the nationalists whom he had defended. Appealing to the Constitution as the protector of minority rights, he developed his principle of state interposition, or nullification. After Calhoun delivered his "Address on the Relations of the States and the Federal Government," Governor James Hamilton of South Carolina asked for clarification of that principle. The following excerpt is from Calhoun's reply to Governor Hamilton. ☐ Richard K. Crallé, Editor, *Reports and Public Letters of John C. Calhoun,* Volume 6, pp. 147–152. New York: D. Appleton and Company, copyright © 1855.

From the beginning, and in all the changes of political existence through which we have passed, the people of the United States have been united as forming political communities, and not as individuals. Even in the first stage of existence, they formed distinct colonies, independent of each other, and politically united only through the British crown. In their first imperfect union, for the purpose of resisting the encroachments of the mother-country, they united as distinct political communities; and, passing from their colonial condition, in the act announcing their independence to the world, they declared themselves, by name and enumeration, free and independent states. In that character, they formed the old confederation; and, when it was proposed to supersede the articles of the confederation by the present Constitution, they met in convention as states, acted and voted as states; and the Constitution, when formed, was submitted for ratification to the people of the several states: it was ratified by them as states, each state for itself; each by its ratification binding its own citizens; the parts thus separately binding themselves, and not the whole the parts; to which, if it be added, that it is declared in the preamble of the Constitution to be ordained by the people of the *United States,* and in the article of ratification, when ratified, it is declared *"to be binding between the states so ratifying."* . . . [The] Constitution is the work of the people of the states, considered as separate and independent political communities; . . . they are its authors—their power created it, their voice clothed it with authority— . . . the government formed is, in reality, their agent; and . . . the Union, of which the Constitution is the bond, is a union of states, and not of individuals. . . .

I will next proceed to state some of the results which necessarily follow from the facts which have been established.

The first, and, in reference to the subject of this communication, the most important, is, that there is *no direct* and *immediate* connexion between the individual citizens of a state and the General [Federal] Government. The relation between them is through the state. The Union is a union of states as communities, and not a union of individuals. As members of a state, her citizens were originally subject to no control but that of the state, and could be subject to no other, except by the act of the state itself. The Constitution was, accordingly, submitted to the states for their separate ratification; and it was only by the ratification of the state that its citizens became subject to the control of the General Government. The ratification of any other, or all the other states, without its own, could create no connexion between them and the General Government, nor impose on them the slightest obligation. Without the ratification of their own state, they would stand in the same relation to the General Government as do the citizens or subjects of any foreign state . . . . It follows, as a necessary consequence, that the act of ratification bound the state as a community, as is expressly declared in the article of the Constitution above quoted, and not the citizens of the state as individuals: the latter being bound through their state, and in consequence of the ratification of the former. Another, and a highly important consequence, as it regards the subject under investigation, follows with equal certainty: that, on a question whether a particular power exercised by the General Government be granted by the Constitution, it belongs to the state as a member of the Union, in her sovereign capacity in convention, to determine definitively, as far as her citizens are concerned, the extent of the obligation which she contracted; and if, in her opinion, the act exercising the power be unconstitutional, to declare it null and void, *which declaration would be obligatory on her citizens.* In coming to this conclusion, it may be proper to remark, to prevent misrepresentation, that I do not claim for a state the right to abrogate an act of the General Government. It is the Constitution that annuls an unconstitutional act. Such an act is of itself void and of no effect. What I claim is, the right of the state, *as far as its citizens are concerned, to declare the extent of the obligation, and that such declaration is binding on them—* a right, when limited to its citizens, flowing directly from the relation of the state to the General Government on the one side, and its citizens on the other, as already explained, and resting on the most plain and solid reasons. . . .

Having now, I trust, established the very important point, that the declaration of a state, as to the extent of the power granted, is obligatory on its citizens, I shall next proceed to consider the effects of such declarations in reference to the General Government: a question which necessarily involves the consideration of the relation between it and the states. It has been shown that the people of the states, acting as distinct and independent communities, are the authors of the Constitution, and that the General Government was organized and ordained by them to execute its powers. The government, then, with all of its departments, is, in fact, the agent of the states, constituted to execute their joint will, as expressed in the Constitution.

In using the term agent, I do not intend to derogate in any degree from its character as a government. It is as truly and properly a government as are the state governments themselves. I have applied it simply because it strictly belongs to the relation between the General Government and the states, as, in fact, it does also to that between a state and its own government. Indeed, according to our theory, governments are in their nature but trusts, and those appointed to administer them trustees or agents to execute the trust powers. The sovereignty resides elsewhere—in the people, not in the government; and with us, *the people* mean *the people of the several states* originally formed into thirteen distinct and independent communities, and now into twenty-four. Politically speaking, in reference to our own system, there are *no other people*. The General Government, as well as those of the states, is but the organ of their power: the latter, that of their respective states, through which are exercised separately that portion of power not delegated by the Constitution, and in the exercise of which each state has a local and peculiar interest; the former, the joint organ of all the states confederated into one general community, and through which they jointly and concurringly exercise the delegated powers, in which all have a common interest. Thus viewed, the Constitution of the United States, with the government it created, is truly and strictly the Constitution of each state, as much so as its own particular Constitution and government, ratified by the same authority, in the same mode, and having, as far as its citizens are concerned, its powers and obligations from the same source, differing only in the aspect, under which I am considering the subject, in the *plighted faith* of the state to its co-states, and of which, as far as its citizens are considered, the state, in the last resort, is the exclusive judge.

# III

## AN ADDRESS TO THE SENATE

The great debate over California statehood in 1850 marked Calhoun's supreme effort to protect the position of the South in the slavery question. The following excerpt consists of portions of his address of March 4, in which he analyzed the plight of the South and offered possible alternatives. □ Richard K. Crallé, Editor, *Speeches of John C. Calhoun*, Volume 4, pp. 542–545, 548–553, 556, 571–573. New York: D. Appleton and Company, copyright © 1854.

I have, Senators, believed from the first that the agitation of the subject of slavery would, if not prevented by some timely and effective measure, end in disunion. Entertaining this opinion, I have, on all proper occasions, endeavored to call the attention of both the two great parties which divide the country to adopt some measure to prevent so great a disaster, but without success. The agitation has been permitted to proceed, with almost no attempt to resist it, until it has reached a point when it can no longer be disguised or denied that the Union is in danger. You have thus had forced upon you the greatest and the gravest question that can ever come under your consideration—How can the Union be preserved? . . .

The first question . . . presented for consideration, in the investigation I propose to make, in order to obtain such knowledge, is—What is it that has endangered the Union? . . .

One of the causes is, undoubtedly, to be traced to the long-continued agitation of the slave question on the part of the North, and the many aggressions which they have made on the rights of the South during the time. . . .

There is another lying back of it—with which this is intimately connected—that may be regarded as the great and primary cause. This is to be found in the fact that the equilibrium between the two sections, in the Government as it stood when the constitution was ratified and the Government put in action, has been destroyed. At that time there was nearly a perfect equilibrium between the two, which afforded ample means to each to protect itself against the aggression of the other; but, as it now stands, one section has the exclusive power of controlling the Government, which leaves the other without any adequate means of protecting itself against its encroachment and oppression. . . .

. . . [The] United States, since they declared their independence, have acquired 2,373,046 square miles of territory, from which the North will have excluded the South, if she should succeed in monopolizing the newly acquired territories, about three-fourths of the whole, leaving to the South but about one-fourth.

Such is the first and great cause that has destroyed the equilibrium between the two sections in the Government.

The next is the system of revenue and disbursements which has been adopted by the Government. It is well known that the Government has derived its revenue mainly from duties on imports. I shall not undertake to show that such duties must necessarily fall mainly on the exporting States, and that the South, as the great exporting portion of the Union, has

in reality paid vastly more than her due proportion of the revenue . . . .
Nor shall I . . . undertake to show that a far greater portion of the revenue
has been disbursed at the North, than its due share; and that the joint
effect of these causes has been, to transfer a vast amount from South
to North . . . . If to this be added, that many of the duties were imposed,
not for revenue, but for protection,—that is, intended to put money, not
in the treasury, but directly into the pocket of the manufacturers,—
some conception may be formed of the immense amount which, in the
long course of sixty years, has been transferred from South to North. . . .
Under the most moderate estimate, it would be sufficient to add greatly
to the wealth of the North, and thus greatly increase her population
by attracting emigration from all quarters to that section.

This, combined with the great primary cause, amply explains why
the North has acquired a preponderance in every department of the Government by its disproportionate increase of population and States. . . .
The loss, then, of the equilibrium is to be attributed to the action of this
Government.

But while these measures were destroying the equilibrium between
the two sections, the action of the Government was leading to a radical
change in its character, by concentrating all the power of the system in
itself. . . .

That the Government claims, and practically maintains the right to
decide in the last resort, as to the extent of its powers, will scarcely be
denied by any one conversant with the political history of the country.
That it also claims the right to resort to force to maintain whatever power
it claims, against all opposition, is equally certain. . . . Now, I ask, what
limitation can possibly be placed upon the powers of a government claiming and exercising such rights? And, if none can be, how can the separate
governments of the States maintain and protect the powers reserved to
them by the constitution—or the people of the several States maintain
those which are reserved to them? . . . It also follows, that the character
of the Government has been changed in consequence, from a federal
republic, as it originally came from the hands of its framers, into a great
national consolidated democracy. . . .

The result of the whole of these causes combined is—that the North
has acquired a decided ascendency over every department of this Government, and through it a control over all the powers of the system. A
single section governed by the will of the numerical majority, has now, in
fact, the control of the Government and the entire powers of the system.
What was once a constitutional federal republic, is now converted, in

reality, into one as absolute as that of the Autocrat of Russia, and as despotic in its tendency as any absolute government that ever existed. . . .

. . . [If] there was no question of vital importance to the South, in reference to which there was a diversity of views between the two sections, this state of things might be endured, without the hazard of destruction to the South. But such is not the fact. There is a question of vital importance to the Southern section, in reference to which the views and feelings of the two sections are as opposite and hostile as they can possibly be.

I refer to the relation between the two races in the Southern section, which constitutes a vital portion of her social organization. Every portion of the North entertains views and feelings more or less hostile to it. . . . On the contrary, the Southern section regards the relation as one which cannot be destroyed without subjecting the two races to the greatest calamity, and the section to poverty, desolation, and wretchedness; and accordingly they feel bound, by every consideration of interest and safety, to defend it.

This hostile feeling on the part of the North towards the social organization of the South long lay dormant, but it only required some cause to act on those who felt most intensely that they were responsible for its continuance, to call it into action. The increasing power of this Government, and of the control of the Northern section over all its departments, furnished the cause. It was this which made an impression on the minds of many, that there was little or no restraint to prevent the Government from doing whatever it might choose to do. This was sufficient of itself to put the most fanatical portion of the North in action, for the purpose of destroying the existing relation between the two races in the South. . . .

Such is a brief history of the agitation, as far as it has yet advanced. Now I ask, Senators, what is there to prevent its further progress, until it fulfills the ultimate end proposed, unless some decisive measure should be adopted to prevent it? Has any one of the causes, which has added to its increase from its original small and contemptible beginning until it has attained its present magnitude, diminished in force? Is the original cause of the movement—that slavery is a sin, and ought to be suppressed—weaker now than at the commencement? Or is the abolition party less numerous or influential, or have they less influence with, or control over the two great parties of the North in elections? Or has the South greater means of influencing or controlling the movements of this Government now, than it had when the agitation commenced? To all these questions but one answer can be given: No—no—no. The very reverse is true. Instead of being weaker, all the elements in favor of agitation are stronger now than they were in 1835, when it first commenced, while all the elements of influence on the part of the South are weaker. Unless something decisive is done, I again ask, what is to stop this agitation, before the great and final object at which it aims—the abolition of slavery in the States—is consummated? Is it, then, not certain, that if something is not done to arrest it, the South will be forced to choose between abolition and secession? Indeed, as events are now moving, it will not require the South to secede, in order to dissolve the Union. Agitation will of itself effect it . . . .

. . . I return to the question with which I commenced, How can the Union be saved? There is but one way by which it can with any certainty; and that is, by a full and final settlement, on the principle of justice, of all the questions at issue between the two sections. The South asks for justice, simple justice, and less she ought not to take. . . . [By] satisfying the South, she could remain honorably and safely in the Union, and thereby restore the harmony and fraternal feelings between the sections . . . .

But can this be done? Yes, easily; not by the weaker party, for it can of itself do nothing—not even protect itself—but by the stronger. The North has only to will it to accomplish it—to do justice by conceding to the South an equal right in the acquired territory, and to do her duty by causing the stipulations relative to fugitive slaves to be faithfully fulfilled—to cease the agitation of the slave question, and to provide for the insertion of a provision in the constitution, by an amendment, which will restore to the South, in substance, the power she possessed of protecting herself, before the equilibrium between the sections was destroyed by the action of this Government. . . .

But will the North agree to this? It is for her to answer the question. . . . [The] responsibility of saving the Union rests on the North, and not on the South. . . .

. . . If you, who represent the stronger portion, cannot agree to settle. . . [these differences] on the broad principle of justice and duty, say so; and let the States we both represent agree to separate and part in peace. If you are unwilling we should part in peace, tell us so, and we shall know what to do, when you reduce the question to submission or resistance. If you remain silent, you will compel us to infer by your acts what you intend. In that case, California will become the test question. If you admit her, under all the difficulties that oppose her admission, you compel us to infer that you intend to exclude us from the whole of the acquired territories, with the intention of destroying, irretrievably, the equilibrium between the two sections. We would be blind not to perceive in that case, that your real objects are power and aggrandizement, and infatuated not to act accordingly.

I have now, Senators, done my duty in expressing my opinions fully, freely, and candidly, on this solemn occasion. . . . I have exerted myself, during the whole period, to arrest it [the agitation of the slavery question], with the intention of saving the Union, if it could be done; and if it could not, to save the section where it has pleased Providence to cast my lot, and which I sincerely believe has justice and the constitution on its side. Having faithfully done my duty to the best of my ability, both to the Union and my section, throughout this agitation, I shall have the consolation, let what will come, that I am free from all responsibility.

PROBLEM 5

# John Quincy Adams:
# Independent

Political leaders work to establish and maintain a strong and active public following, ensuring their continued re-election. They must be aware of the views of their constituents in order to be successful as leaders. Conscious of this fact, many elected officials have office staffs which help them communicate effectively with the voters. The staff members schedule appearances at many public ceremonies. They write speeches, answer letters, send out newsletters, and advise office holders on entertaining constituents. No political leader today can act without regard for the opinions of the people in his district, but this concern for popular support has not always been so strong.

Until the passage of the Seventeenth Amendment in 1912, United States Senators were elected by the members of the state legislatures. Similarly, until 1915, when some form of the direct primary election had been adopted by every state, parties controlled selection of candidates. Elected officials were responsible only to the party bosses and state legislators. If a politician sought favor, keeping the good will of these men was probably easier than maintaining sound relationships with all the people of a state.

John Quincy Adams sought favor from neither the people nor the political bosses. He voted on the issues of the day as he alone saw fit, believing that he was not in office merely to reflect the views of his constituents. While Adams recognized that his attitude might cost him the support of the voters, he preferred retiring from office to compromising his beliefs.

Adams held a greater number of important political offices than any other person in the history of the United States. He was Minister to the Hague, Emissary to England, Minister to Prussia, state senator, United States Senator, Minister to Russia, head of the American Mission to negotiate peace with England, Minister to England, Secretary of State, President of the United States, and member of the House of Representatives. Talented and brilliant though he was, he lacked many of the personal attributes which make a politician attractive to either the voters or the political bosses. Because he was so unbending and independent, Adams met defeat in attempts at re-election to the United States Senate in 1808 and to the presidency in 1828. However, his understanding and conduct of foreign relations was recognized by his appointments to important positions in the State Department.

Finally achieving the status of elder statesman, in his election to the United States House of Representatives in 1830, Adams was admired by friend and foe alike for his stubborn adherence to principle. James Truslow Adams, a modern biographer of the New England Adams family, though not a member of it, has viewed John Quincy Adams at the time of his resignation from the United States Senate and described his later role in Congress. While John Quincy did not consider himself an eloquent man, James Truslow explains, "The day was to come . . . when he would be heard as the voice of the prophet [foreseeing the role of slavery in bringing on the Civil War], but it would be due to the utter selflessness and intensity of opinions to which he would give utterance rather than to the rhetoric in which they would be clothed."

The excerpt in Problem 5 concerns only one part of Adams' long career in government. It comes from the late President John F. Kennedy's book *Profiles in Courage,* which was awarded the 1957 Pulitzer Prize for biography.

As you read the excerpt, keep the following questions in mind:

**1**    What were Adams' outstanding character traits? What elements of his background helped to form his character?

**2**    What did Adams hope to accomplish in politics? How did his character traits help him to achieve his goals? How did they hinder him?

**3**    Compare John Quincy Adams and John C. Calhoun as United States Senators. What group of people supported Adams? What did they hope to gain through him? What group of people supported Calhoun? What did they hope to gain through him?

**4**    What does this reading reveal about the role of the independent in politics? How did Adams feel about his role as an independent at the end of his life?

## THE INDEPENDENT AS A LEADER

To illustrate John Quincy Adams' independent leadership, John F. Kennedy focused his Adams narrative in *Profiles in Courage* on the years which Adams spent in the United States Senate, from 1803 to 1808. It was during his time as a United States Senator that Adams reaffirmed the position of political independence which he took while a state senator in Massachusetts. This independence characterized his entire career.  ☐  John F. Kennedy, *Profiles in Courage*, pp. 37–51. New York: Harper & Row, Publishers. Copyright © 1956 by John F. Kennedy.

The story of the son is not wholly separable from the story of the father. For John Quincy Adams was, as Samuel Eliot Morison has described him, "above all an Adams"; and his heartwarming devotion to his father and the latter's steadfast loyalty to his son regardless of political embarrassment offer a single ray of warmth in that otherwise hard, cold existence. ("What a queer family!" Federalist leader Harrison Otis wrote in later years, "I think them all varieties in a peculiar species of our race exhibiting a combination of talents and good moral character with passions and prejudices calculated to defeat their own objects and embarrass their friends.") As a child in a tightly knit Puritan family, John Quincy had been taught by his mother to emulate his famous father; and as a Senator, when colleagues and friends deserted him on every side, it was to his father that he turned for support and approval.

Even after the death of the elder Adams, John Quincy maintained touching loyalty to his father's memory. Reading in Jefferson's works the letters written by the latter more than thirty-five years earlier when his father and Jefferson had been political rivals (although their early friendship was later revived), he could still work himself into a rage at what he regarded as Jefferson's perfidy. "His treatment of my father," Adams wrote in his diary, "was double-dealing, treacherous and false beyond all toleration." John Quincy did not comprehend, after a lifetime in the thick of it, how our complicated Federal system of checks and balances operated; nor did he realize that what he regarded as Jefferson's "machinations" was merely a facet of the latter's genius applied with success to the art and science of Government.

The failure of John Quincy Adams to recognize the political facts of life first became apparent during his years in the Senate, years which were neither the most productive of his life nor those in which his contribution was especially significant. Yet his single term in the United States Senate gives us a clear insight into the fate of a man who brought to the public service notable faculties, a respected name and a singular ambition for the right. His experience illustrates as does almost none other that even this extraordinary equipment is not enough to succeed in American political life.

It was not unnatural that John Quincy, returning to Boston after diplomatic service abroad upon his father's defeat for President by Thomas Jefferson, should become active in the affairs of his father's party. He admired the Federalists as the founders of the Constitution, the champions of naval power and a bulwark against French Revolutionary influences.

But no sooner had the young ex-diplomat been elected as a Federalist to the Massachusetts legislature [1802] when he demonstrated his audacious disdain for narrow partisanship. Without consulting his senior colleagues, he proposed—only forty-eight hours after he had become a member of that august legislative body—that the Republican (Jeffersonian or Democratic) party be given proportional representation on the Governor's council. (Adams later noted that this act of non-partisan independence "marked the principle by which my whole public life has been governed from that day to this.")

In subsequently selecting young Adams for the Senate, his colleagues in the state legislature may have assumed that the honor for one of his comparative youth would help impress upon him his obligations to his party. . . .

Arriving in Washington, Adams promptly indicated his disregard for both party affiliations and customary freshman reticence. Although illness in the family had prevented him from arriving in time to vote on ratification of President Jefferson's treaty for the purchase of the Louisiana Territory, he promptly aroused a storm of controversy by becoming the only Federalist to support that precedent-shattering acquisition actively on the floor and to vote for an $11 million appropriation to effectuate it. His democratic principles also caused him to fight administration measures for imposing a government and taxes upon the residents of the Territory—thus incurring the opposition of his Republican colleagues as well. But, with a vision of an America stretched to its continental limits, he regarded Jefferson's remarkable feat in excluding Napoleon from our boundaries while enriching our nation as far more important than the outraged astonishment of his Federalist colleagues. Concerned primarily with maintaining the hegemony [leadership] of New England, they feared westward expansion would diminish the political and economic influence of the commercial cities of the Northeast, lower the value of Eastern lands in which they were financially interested, and provide the Jeffersonians with a permanent majority in Congress. The young Federalist from Massachusetts, as though he were oblivious to their attitude, heaped fuel upon the fires of Federalist rage by attending a banquet of Jeffersonians in celebration of the purchase!

"The dinner was bad and the toasts too numerous," Adams complained dourly in his diary that night. But it is doubtful that even a feast reminiscent of Boston's finest inns would have made his attendance worth while—for this was regarded by his Federalist friends as the final proof of perfidy.

"Curse on the stripling, how he apes his sire!" wrote Theodore Lyman, a prominent Federalist who had sided with Pickering in the latter's falling-out with the senior Adams. But there was only one Federalist politician whose opinion young John Quincy valued above his own—John Adams. Anxiously, he sought his father's views, and the reassurance he received from that elder statesman early in 1804 compensated for all the abuse he had received at the hands of his father's party. "I do not disapprove of your conduct in the business of Louisiana," John Adams wrote his son, "though I know it will become a very unpopular subject in the northern states.... I think you have been right!"

In his diary young Adams summed up his first months in the Senate: "I have already had occasion to experience, which I had before the fullest reason to expect, the danger of adhering to my own principles. The country is so totally given up to the spirit of party that not to follow blindfolded the one or the other is an expiable offence. . . . Between both [parties], I see the impossibility of pursuing the dictates of my own conscience without sacrificing every prospect, not merely of advancement, but even of retaining that character and reputation I have enjoyed. Yet my choice is made, and, if I cannot hope to give satisfaction to my country, I am at least determined to have the approbation of my own reflections."

The possession of the proud name of Adams could not prevent—and may well have hastened—the young Senator's gradual emergence as a minority of one. Had his political philosophy been more popular, his personal mannerisms would still have made close alliances difficult. He was, after all, "an Adams . . . cold, tactless and rigidly conscientious." The son of an unpopular father, a renegade in his party and rather brash for a freshman Senator, John Quincy neither sought nor was offered political alliances or influence.

After only ten days in the Senate he had irritated his seniors and precipitated a three-hour debate by objecting to a routine resolution calling upon Senators to wear crepe one month in honor of three recently deceased patriots. Such a resolution, he somewhat impertinently argued, was improper if not unconstitutional by "tending to unsuitable discussions of character, and to debates altogether foreign to the subjects which properly belong" in the Senate. Next he astounded his colleagues by seeking to disqualify from an impeachment hearing any Senator who had previously voted on the impeachment resolution as a Member of the House. Then to show his stubborn intellectual independence, he alone opposed a motion to go into executive session when its sole purpose, he thought, was to give in the *Journal* an appearance of doing business when actually there was none to be done.

But if the Federalist party learned to dislike the "stripling" even more intensely than they had disliked "his sire," it must be said that any Federalist love for John Quincy would have been wasted anyway. For he became increasingly contemptuous of the Federalist party. An American nationalist who had lived a great part of his brief life abroad, he could not yield his devotion to the national interest for the narrowly partisan, parochial and pro-British outlook which dominated New England's first political party. His former colleagues in the State Legislature publicly charged him with ungrateful "conduct worthy of Machiavelli"; but he wrote his mother that he felt that, as Senator, he could best determine what Massachusetts' best interests were, and "if Federalism consists in looking to the British navy as the only palladium of our liberty, I must be a political heretic."

Many Senators before and after 1804 have combatted the ill-effects of being termed a political heretic by their party chieftains by building strong personal popularity among their constituents. This became increasingly possible as universal manhood suffrage became general early in the nineteenth century. But not John Quincy Adams. He regarded every public measure that came before him, a fellow Senator observed, as though it were an abstract proposition from Euclid, unfettered by considerations of political appeal. He denied the duty of elected representatives "to be palsied by the will of their constituents"; and he refused to achieve success by becoming what he termed a "patriot by profession," by pretending "extraordinary solicitude for the people, by flattering their prejudices, by ministering to their passions, and by humoring their transient and changeable opinions." His guiding star was the principle of Puritan statesmanship his father had laid down many years before: *The magistrate is the servant not of his own desires, not even of the people, but of his God."*

We would admire the courage and determination of John Quincy Adams if he served in the Senate today. We would respect his nonpartisan, nonsectional approach. But I am not so certain that we would like him as a person; and it is apparent that many of his colleagues, on both sides of the aisle, did not. His isolation from either political party, and the antagonisms which he aroused, practically nullified the impact of his own independent and scholarly propositions. His diary reveals that the young Senator was not wholly insensitive to his increasing political isolation: he complained that he had "nothing to do but to make fruitless opposition." "I have already seen enough to ascertain that no amendments of my proposing will obtain in the Senate as now filled." "I have no doubt of incurring much censure and obloquy for this measure." And he referred to those "who hate me rather more than they love any principle." He was particularly bitter about Pickering's contemptuous conduct toward him, and felt that his colleague "abandons altogether the ground of right, and relies upon what is expedient."

But it was not until 1807 that the split between party and Senator became irreparable, and Adams was denounced by the great majority of his constituents, as well as the party chiefs. The final break, naturally enough, concerned this nation's foreign policy. As our relations with Great Britain worsened, our ships were seized, our cargoes were confiscated, and our seamen were "impressed" by British cruisers and compelled to serve—as alleged British subjects—in the King's navy. Thousands of American seamen were taken on an organized basis, ships were lost at sea for want of men, and even those able to "prove" American citizenship were frequently refused permission to return. Adams' patriotic instincts were aroused, and he was indignant that the very Federalist merchants whose ships were attacked had decided that appeasement of Great Britain was the only answer to their problems. His Federalist colleagues even attempted to rationalize such aggressive measures by talking vaguely of Britain's difficulties in her war with France and our friendly tone toward the latter. With undisguised contempt for this attitude, Adams in 1806 had introduced and pushed to passage—successfully —a unique experience for him, he noted in his diary—a series of resolutions condemning British aggressions upon American ships, and requesting the President to demand restoration and indemnification of the confiscated vessels. The Federalists, of course, had solidly opposed his measures, as they did an Adams-supported administration bill limiting British imports. He was now, for all practical purposes, a man without a party.

Finally, in the summer of 1807, the American frigate *Chesapeake* was summarily fired upon off the Virginia Capes by the British man-of-war *Leopard,* after the American vessel had refused either to be searched or to hand over four seamen whom the English claimed to be British subjects. Several of the American crew were killed or injured. The incensed Adams was convinced that, party or no party, the time for forceful action against such intolerable acts had come. He pleaded with local Federalist officials to call a town meeting in Boston to protest the incident. Turned down, and outraged when a prominent Federalist attempted to justify even the *Leopard's* attack, he discovered to his grim satisfaction that the Republican party was organizing a similar mass meeting to be held at the State House that very week.

The Federalist *Repertory* [a Boston newspaper] warned the faithful that the meeting represented nothing but an "irregular and tumultuous mode of proceeding," which "no just or honorable man" should attend. But John Quincy Adams did attend; and, although he declined to serve as moderator, he nevertheless was instrumental in drafting the group's fighting resolution which pledged to the President the lives and fortunes of the participants in support of "any measures, however serious."

Now the Federalists were outraged. Although they hurriedly called an official town meeting to pledge hypocritically their support to the President too, they stated publicly that John Quincy Adams, for his public association with Republican meetings and causes, should "have his head taken off for apostasy . . . and should no longer be considered as having any communion with the party." It was this episode, the Senator later commented, "which alienated me from that day and forever from the councils of the Federalist party."

When Jefferson on September 18, 1807, called upon Congress to retaliate against the British by enacting an embargo effectively shutting off all further international trade—a measure apparently ruinous to

Massachusetts, the leading commercial state in the nation—it was John Quincy Adams of Massachusetts who rose on the Senate floor and called for referral of the message to a select committee; who was appointed Chairman of the committee; and who reported both the Embargo Bill and a bill of his own preventing British vessels from entering American waters.

"This measure will cost you and me our seats," young Adams remarked to a colleague, as the select committee completed its work and its members made their way to the Senate floor, "but private interest must not be put in opposition to public good."

His words were unerringly prophetic. As the Embargo Bill, with his help, became law, a storm of protest arose in Massachusetts reminiscent of the days of the Boston Tea Party. In that state were located a substantial proportion of America's merchant fleet and practically all of the shipbuilding and fishing industries. The embargo completely idled the shipbuilding industry, destroyed the shipping trade and tied up the fishing vessels; and stagnation, bankruptcy, distress, and migration from the territory became common. Neither merchants nor seamen could be convinced that the act was for their own good. Even the farmers of New England found their products a glut on the market, their export outlets having been closed.

The Federalist leaders insisted the Embargo was an attempt by Jefferson to ruin New England prosperity, to provoke England to war, and to aid the French. Even though New England Republicans refused to defend their President's bill, the Federalist party . . . returned triumphantly to power in both Houses of the Massachusetts legislature. Talk of New England seceding became commonplace.

But however great their hatred for Jefferson and his Embargo, Massachusetts Federalists, merchants and other citizens were even more bitter over the "desertion" of their Senator to the ranks of the enemy. "A party scavenger!" snorted the Northampton *Hampshire Gazette,* "one of those ambitious politicians who lives on both land and water, and occasionally resorts to each, but who finally settles down in the mud." Adams, said the Salem *Gazette,* is "a popularity seeker . . . courting the prevailing party," and one of "Bonaparte's Senators." The Greenfield *Gazette* called him an apostate "associated with the assassins of his father's character." His own social circles in Boston—the rich, the cultivated and the influential—all turned against him. "I would not sit at the same table with that renegade," retorted one of Boston's leading citizens in refusing to attend a dinner at which Adams would be present.

And a leading Federalist wrote with glee to the Washington party stalwarts, "He walks into State Street at the usual hour but seems totally unknown."

John Quincy Adams was alone—but not quite alone. "Most completely was I deserted by my friends, in Boston and in the state legislature," he wrote his mother. "I can never be sufficiently grateful to Providence that my father and my mother did not join in this general desertion." For when the unmerciful abuse from his home state was first heaped upon him, John Quincy had again turned to his father and poured out his feelings. And his father replied that his son's situation was "clear, plain and obvious":

"You are supported by no party; you have too honest a heart, too independent a mind, and too brilliant talents, to be sincerely and confidentially trusted by any man who is under the domination of party maxims or party feelings. . . . You may depend upon it then that your fate is decided. . . . You ought to know and expect this and by no means regret it. My advice to you is steadily to pursue the course you are in, with moderation and caution however, because I think it the path of justice."

But the entire Adams family was damned in the eyes of the ex-President's former supporters by his son's act of courage. "His [John Quincy's] apostasy is no longer a matter of doubt with anybody," cried Representative Gardenier of New York. "I wish to God that the noble house of Braintree [birthplace of Adams in Massachusetts] had been put in a hole—and a deep one, too—20 years ago!" But father and son, the Adamses stood together. "Parton has denounced you as No Federalist," his father wrote, "and I wish he would denounce me in the same manner, for I have long since renounced, abdicated, and disclaimed the name and character and attributes of that sect, as it now appears."

With his father's support—in a fight where he stood with the President who had defeated his father!—John Quincy maintained the unflinching and inflexible bearing which became his Puritan ancestry. When he was accosted in Boston by a politically minded preacher who assailed his views "in a rude and indecent manner, I told him that in consideration of his age I should only remark that he had one lesson yet to learn—Christian charity." When his colleague Pickering denounced him in an open letter to the Legislature which was distributed throughout Massachusetts in tens of thousands, he wrote a masterful reply—criticizing the Federalist party as sectional, outmoded and unpatriotic; insisting that the critical issues of war and peace could not be decided on the basis of "geographical position, party bias or professional occupation"; and exploding at Pickering's servile statement that "Although Great Britain, with her thousand ships of war, could have destroyed our commerce, she has really done it no essential injury."

The Federalist Legislature convened at the end of May 1808, with—as the Massachusetts Republican Governor wrote Jefferson—but one "principal object—the political and even the personal destruction of John Quincy Adams." As soon as both Houses had organized, the legislature immediately elected Adams' successor—nine months prior to the expiration of his term! And as its next order of business, the Legislature promptly passed resolutions instructing its Senators to urge repeal of the Embargo.

"The election," Adams realized, "was precipitated for the sole purpose of specially marking me. For it ought, in regular order, not to have been made until the winter session of the legislature." And the resolutions, he felt, enjoined "upon their Senators a course of conduct which neither my judgment could approve nor my spirit brook."

Only one course was conscientiously open to him—he resigned his seat in the Senate in order to defend the policies of the man who had driven his father from the Presidency.

It was "out of the question," he wrote, to hold his seat "without exercising the most perfect freedom of agency, under the sole and exclusive control of my own sense of right."

"I will only add, that, far from regretting any one of those acts for which I have suffered, I would do them over again, were they now to be done, at the hazard of ten times as much slander, unpopularity, and displacement."

But had his own vote in the Senate been necessary to save Jefferson's foreign policy, Adams wrote to those who criticized his departure at such a critical time, then "highly as I reverenced the authority of my constituents, and bitter as would have been the cup of resistance to their declared will . . . I would have defended their interests against their inclinations, and incurred every possible addition to their resentment, to save them from the vassalage of their own delusions."

Hated by the Federalists and suspected by the Republicans, John Quincy Adams returned to private life. His star was soon to rise again; but he never forgot this incident or abandoned his courage of conscience. (Legend has it that during Adams' politically independent term as President, in response to the Presidential toast "May he strike confusion to his foes!" Daniel Webster dryly commented, "As he has already done to his friends.") Soon after his retirement from the White House in 1829, Adams was asked by the voters of the Plymouth District to represent them in Congress. In disregard of the advice of his family and friends and his own desire for leisure time to write his father's biography, he agreed to accept the post if elected. But he specified, first, that he should never be expected to promote himself as a candidate and ask for votes; and, secondly, that he would pursue a course in Congress completely independent of the party and people who elected him. On this basis Adams was elected by an overwhelming vote, and served in the House until his death. Here he wrote perhaps the brightest chapter of his history, for as "Old Man Eloquent" he devoted his remarkable prestige and tireless energies to the struggle against slavery.

To be returned on this independent basis to the Congress from which he had departed so ignominiously twenty-two years earlier was a deeply moving experience for the courageous ex-Senator. "I am a member-elect of the Twenty-Second Congress," he recorded with pride in his diary. "No election or appointment conferred upon me ever gave me so much pleasure. My election as President of the United States was not half so gratifying to my inmost soul."

PROBLEM 6

# James K. Polk:
# Success in the Presidency

Why does one President succeed in achieving his goals and another fail? If this question had a simple answer, clear guidelines could be set up for voters, who then might be better able to make choices.

Two major elements determine the success or failure of a President. One of these elements involves the reputation, personality, and talents of the man himself. If he has a capacity for compromise and for persuading men of diverse views to work together for a common cause, he possesses a valuable advantage. On the whole, Presidents who welded effective coalitions behind their policies were more successful than those who could not induce rivals to forget differences. A President has an additional advantage if he assumes office, as George Washington did, with his reputation for leadership firmly established.

Conditions under which a President holds power are a second element which determines his success or failure. Some chief executives had a Congress controlled overwhelmingly by men of their own parties; others faced hostility from legislatures dominated by members of the opposition. During some periods great questions divided the nation and frustrated the President's plans; in others most people united for common programs.

James K. Polk had both elements working against him. He was not well known to the majority of voters when the Democrats nominated him for the presidency in 1844. In fact, he had been chosen as the nominee only after rival factions failed to agree on other candidates. He is often described as the first "dark horse" in presidential history. "Who is James K. Polk?" asked his Whig opponents. Some of them knew him better than they admitted, for Polk had been in politics all his life. He served four years as Speaker of the United States House of Representatives and two years as governor of Tennessee. However, those persons who did not know him as well were unable to point to a conspicuous record or to personal qualities that were outstanding.

Nor were the times promising. Divided over issues such as slavery, the tariff, and United States policy concerning Mexico, voters and politicians were not likely to form a united front. Yet, despite these handicaps, Polk achieved his goals. Part of his success may be attributed to the fact that he entered office with a definite program, which he was determined to have written into law.

The task of accomplishing this program required his constant attention: he was absent from Washington for only six weeks in four years. Three months after he left office, James Polk was dead.

The first reading in Problem 5 places Polk among the ten greatest Presidents of the United States. It analyzes Polk's ability as a leader and provides insight into the political climate of the period. The second reading, an excerpt from Polk's diary, indicates the strategy he employed in declaring war on Mexico.

As you read, consider these questions:

1    What were Polk's main personal characteristics? What were his political goals?

2    What was the political atmosphere in which Polk worked? What was the nature of his opposition?

3    Given Polk's personal attributes and the situation in which he worked, how do you account for his success?

# I

## WHO IS JAMES K. POLK?

A modern historian, Norman A. Graebner, seeks an understanding of James K. Polk's success as a political leader and as President. In analyzing Polk's character, he presents a concise view of the complex problems of his administration; and he explains the man's energy in accepting the responsibilities of his office. Portions of Graebner's work make up the reading which follows. ☐ Norman A. Graebner, "James Polk." Morton Borden, Editor, *America's Ten Greatest Presidents,* pp. 113–120. Chicago: Rand McNally & Company, copyright © 1961.

"Who is James K. Polk?" demanded the Whigs contemptuously of their Democratic opponents during the presidential canvass of 1844. In feigning astonishment at the Democratic choice, these men were exploiting a dilemma which long characterized Polk's political career. Except among his close associates he was unloved and unappreciated in his own day; throughout the nineteenth century Americans all but ignored him. Perhaps the reason is clear. Men are remembered for their unique qualities, and Polk had none. In oratory he lacked the elegance of Daniel Webster; in intellect, the preciseness of John C. Calhoun. In reputation he was no match for the Whig party's gallant hero, Henry Clay. Not even in personality or appearance was he conspicuous. He was below average in height, with thin face and piercing grey eyes. He wore his hair long and brushed back behind his ears. He was an uncompromising Presbyterian — a man honest and incorruptible, thoughtful and meditative, slow and measured in speech, methodical and industrious. Polk's personal attributes were worthy, even admirable, but they hardly conveyed distinction. . . .

Polk had more than experience and an ambitious party bloc behind him. He had an unsuspected feel for leadership. He accepted the dictum of Alexander Hamilton that the American system provides no substitute for energy in the executive. Not long after he entered the presidency, one Washington editor said of him: "Few men are capable of the labors which he encounters; and few in his place would devote themselves with the same assiduity to the public service. He works from 10 to 12 hours in every 24. He holds two Cabinets a week. He sees visitors two hours every day when the Cabinet is not employed. . . . He is also in frequent communion with his secretaries." . . .

Polk was guide and master of his administration. Ten weeks before his inauguration he wrote to Cave Johnson of Tennessee, later to become his postmaster general, ". . . I intend to be myself President of the United States." Polk demanded absolute cooperation from members of his Cabinet, and required assurances that they would retire at the moment they became aspirants for the presidency. For Polk this appeared essential, for his announcement, at the time of his nomination, that he would not seek re-election raised the issue of the succession even before he entered the White House. In Cabinet sessions Polk encouraged free discussion. He listened attentively, but seldom abandoned his convictions. Gideon Welles, never an admirer of the President, reported early in Polk's administration that several Cabinet members "have been at particular pains to tell me that the President has his own way . . . does as he had a mind to." [Welles was a Jacksonian Democrat who in 1861 became Secretary of the Navy in Abraham Lincoln's cabinet.] Later the reluctant Welles admitted that Polk "had courage and determination and shrank from no labor or responsibility." Judge John Catron wrote to Andrew Jackson in the spring of 1845: "Our friend is very prudent, and *eminently* firm, regardless of consequences. He came here to be—THE PRESIDENT— which at this date is as undisputed as that you was The GENL at N. Orleans." Jackson discovered how little he could influence Polk when the new President, ignoring the General's admonition, removed Francis P. Blair and the *Globe,* and established the Washington *Union* under Thomas Ritchie as the official organ of the Administration.

George Bancroft, the eminent historian and Polk's first secretary of the navy, has left the most impressive testimony of Polk's administrative capacity. Fifty years after the events of the 1840's he recalled that Polk, on his inauguration day, informed him that he had four key objectives as President: tariff reduction, re-establishment of the Independent Treasury, the settlement of the Oregon boundary, and the acquisition of California. That Polk achieved these goals led Bancroft to the conclusion that he was "one of the very foremost of our public men and one of the very best and most honest and most successful Presidents the country ever had." Polk's administration succeeded, Bancroft added, "because he insisted on being its centre, and in overruling and guiding all his secretaries to act so as to produce unity and harmony."

Polk's rigid control of his administrative machinery accounts only partially for his success. Every aspect of his program required the eventual approval of Congress. That he achieved Congressional majorities on his pet measures has been written off by some historians as a simple expression of public opinion. Had he tried to dominate Congress, say his critics, his lack of color would have proved fatal. Only as a mirror of Jacksonianism was he equal to the task. But public opinion is never clearly defined or easily converted into policy. Polk's Democratic party was no longer united in 1845 on any philosophy. Throughout the expanding industrial and commercial centers of the North were powerful Democratic voices which sounded less and less Jacksonian as they demanded that the Federal government underwrite the economy with a variety of special dispensations. In both houses of Congress were determined Whig minorities that maintained a persistent attack on Polk's leadership. Against his enemies the President commanded the allegiance of only a segment of the party which had elected him.

Van Buren's followers were sullen. Since the Texas issue had carried Polk into the White House, they predicted logically that the friends of annexation would dominate the new administration. When Polk's Cabinet appointments favored "Texas" men, the Van Burenites concluded that the President had sold out to their enemies. . . .

Neither was Calhoun's powerful Southern faction represented in the Cabinet. . . . Whatever the motive behind the Cabinet appointments, Polk, as president, faced resentment in two of the three important factions of his party. It was doubtful in March, 1845, if the Democratic organization was sufficiently united to carry any measure against a resolute Whig minority. Thomas Corwin, the partisan Ohio Whig, saw the Administration's dilemma clearly. "The truth is," he wrote, "Polk is not far from the category of Tyler. He is like Tyler an accident. He knows this. His friends know & feel it, and if his friends were United they would compel him to many a wild & wicked freak. But his friends are not united."

Polk was unawed by this opposition [from within his own party]. When Congress met in December, 1845, he not only confronted it with a carefully-prepared program but he also made it clear that he was determined to carry this program into law. From the moment that Congress assembled, he exerted continuous pressure on key Democrats in both Houses through personal interviews or through members of the Cabinet. To Polk every administration proposal was a party measure to be forced through Congress as a matter of party responsibility.

Such determination merely reflected the President's deep conviction. Early in his career Polk had imbibed the philosophy of Thomas Jefferson. He entered political life an enemy of Clay's American System, and never ceased to condemn the protective tariff, the national Bank and credit system, internal improvements, and the distribution of Federal surpluses among the states. "I would keep no surplus revenue there to scramble for, either for internal improvements, or for any thing else," he once remarked. "I would bring the Government back to what it was intended to be, a plain economical Government." Even as President he never compromised with these beliefs.

Southern Democrats had led a continuous, if unsuccessful, assault on the high Whig Tariff of 1842. Polk renewed the attack in his message to Congress in December, 1845. He admitted that Congress had the power to levy taxes and could institute a tariff for that purpose. "But care should be taken," he added, "that all the great interests of the country, including manufactures, agriculture, commerce, navigation, and the mechanic arts, should . . . derive equal advantages from the incidental protection which a just system of revenue duties may afford." Taxes, he said, should be imposed on all classes according to their ability to pay. The existing tariff was wrong because it imposed "heavy and unjust burdens on the farmer, the planter, the commercial man, and those of all other pursuits except the capitalist who has made his investments in manufactures." Secretary of the Treasury [Robert J.] Walker prepared the new tariff bill, mildly protective but proposing a general reduction of rates. In addition, the Walker bill introduced a simplified form by separating all dutiable goods into groups and providing *ad valorem* rates for each classification.

Opponents of tariff revision declared repeatedly throughout the ensuing debate that they comprised a majority in Congress, but Polk and Walker, aided by George Dwight, a little-known Massachusetts Whig, maintained a steady pressure on Congress. Dwight occupied a large parlor in one of the capital's leading hotels and there dispensed generous, if discriminate, hospitality as an agent of British manufacturing and mercantile interests. When the President in March learned that the Committee on Ways and Means was prepared to introduce specific duties on iron, he called in its chairman, James I. McKay of North Carolina, and extracted from him a promise to report the bill in its original form. Late in April word reached the White House that the Whigs in the Senate had managed to postpone action on the tariff bill. Polk reminded Dixon H. Lewis, chairman of the Senate Finance Committee, of the recommendations of the annual message. "I told him," the President recorded in his diary, "that I considered them as administration measures and that I intended to urge them upon Congress as such, and that I considered the public good, as well as my own power and the glory of my administration, depended in a great degree upon my success in carrying them through Congress." So occupied was Polk with Congressional affairs that seldom did he miss having evening callers when Congress was in session.

July was the critical month for the tariff. Shortly before the House vote was taken on July 3 the President reminded Daniel Dickinson of New York that the vote would be close and that the fate of the measure lay with the Democratic delegation from his state. Dickinson left immediately for the Capitol while Polk dispatched other members of Congress to exert similar pressure on doubtful votes. That afternoon Dickinson was able to report the successful passage of the bill in the House. The Senate decision remained doubtful. Scores of lobbyists had invaded Washington to defeat the measure. "The absence of a single democratic Senator will probably enable them to effect their object," observed the President. "I considered the passage of the bill before the Senate the most important domestic measure of my administration, and therefore I take so great an interest in it."

So tightly were the lines drawn on the tariff that everyone in Washington knew the Senate decision hinged on every vote. Polk learned that James Semple of Illinois was about to leave Washington on business. After a long conversation Polk secured Semple's agreement to remain. As the Senate vote neared all attention was focused on two men, William H. Haywood of North Carolina and Spencer Jarnagin of Tennessee. Haywood, a Democrat, balked at voting for tariff reduction. Polk warned him that he would be the only Southern Democrat voting against the measure and that he "would strike a severe blow upon my administration, inflict grave injury on the country, and . . . would ruin himself." Haywood resigned his seat rather than vote against his conscience or his party.

Now the fate of the new tariff was in the hands of Jarnagin, a Whig under instructions from the Tennessee legislature to vote for tariff reduction. Polk dispatched Hopkins Turney, a Tennessee Democrat, to encourage Jarnagin to obey his instructions. Webster, leader of the protariff forces in the Senate, brought the full weight of his prestige to bear on Jarnagin, but at the White House the Tennessean promised Polk that he would vote for the Walker bill and thereafter refused to discuss the matter with the Whigs. During the fateful session, Jarnagin stalked from the Senate chamber and permitted Vice President Dallas to cast the deciding vote for engrossment. Then the Tennessee Whig returned to vote for the final passage. Executive leadership was decisive throughout.

# II

## THE DIARY OF A PRESIDENT

James K. Polk kept his diary with great care, making records of many events during his presidency which are useful in understanding his attitudes toward leadership. The entry for May 9, 1846, illustrates the way in which he handled the delicate question of declaring war on Mexico. □ Milo Milton Quaife, Editor, *The Diary of James K. Polk,* Volume 1, pp. 384–387. Chicago: A. C. McClurg & Co., copyright © 1910.

SATURDAY, *9th May, 1846.*—The Cabinet held a regular meeting to-day; all the members present. I brought up the Mexican question, and the question of what was the duty of the administration in the present state of our relations with that country. The subject was very fully discussed. All agreed that if the Mexican forces at Matamoras committed any act of hostility on Gen'l Taylor's forces I should immediately send a message to Congress recommending an immediate declaration of War. I stated to the cabinet that up to this time, as they knew, we had heard of no open act of aggression by the Mexican army, but that the danger was imminent that such acts would be committed. I said that in my opinion we had ample cause of war, and that it was impossible that we could stand in *statu quo,* or that I could remain silent much longer; that I thought it was my duty to send a message to Congress very soon & recommend definitive measures. I told them that I thought I ought to make such a message by tuesday next, that the country was excited and impatient on the subject, and if I failed to do so I would not be doing my duty. I then propounded the distinct question to the Cabinet and took their opinions individually, whether I should make a message to Congress on tuesday, and whether in that message I should recommend a declaration of War against Mexico. All except the Secretary of the Navy gave their advice in the affirmative. Mr. Bancroft dissented but said if any act of hostility should be committed by the Mexican forces he was then in favour of immediate war. Mr. Buchanan said he would feel better satisfied in his course if the Mexican forces had or should commit any act of hostility, but that as matters stood we had ample cause of war against Mexico, & he gave his assent to the measure. It was agreed that the message should be prepared and submitted to the Cabinet in their meeting on tuesday. A history of our causes of complaint against Mexico had been at my request previously drawn up by Mr. Buchanan. I stated that what was said in my annual message in December gave that history as succinctly and satisfactorily as Mr. Buchanan's statement, that in truth it was the same history in both, expressed in different language, and that if I repeated that history in [a] message to Congress now I had better employ the precise language used in my message of December last. Without deciding this point the Cabinet passed to the consideration of some other subjects of minor importance. The Cabinet adjourned about 2 O'Clock P.M. Before they separated I directed the Secretary of State to have all the correspondence of Mr. [John] Slidell [special minister to Mexico] with the Mexican Government, & such portions of his correspondence with the Department of State as it was proper to communicate copied;

and in like manner I directed the Secretary of War to have all his orders to Gen'l Taylor commanding the army in Texas copied, so as to have these documents ready to be communicated to Congress with my message.

About 6 o'clock P.M. Gen'l R. Jones, the Adjutant General of the army, called and handed to me despatches received from Gen'l Taylor by the Southern mail which had just arrived, giving information that a part of [the] Mexican army had crossed . . . the Del Norte, and attacked and killed and captured two companies of dragoons of Gen'l Taylor's army consisting of 63 officers & men. The despatch also stated that he had on that day (26th April) made a requisition on the Governors of Texas and Louisiana for four Regiments each, to be sent to his relief at the earliest practicable period. Before I had finished reading the despatch, the Secretary of War called. I immediately summoned the Cabinet to meet at 7½ O'Clock this evening. The Cabinet accordingly assembled at that hour; all the members present. The subject of the despatch received this evening from Gen'l Taylor, as well as the state of our relations with Mexico, were fully considered. The Cabinet were unanimously of opinion, and it was so agreed, that a message should be sent to Congress on Monday laying all the information in my possession before them and recommending vigorous & prompt measure[s] to enable the Executive to prosecute the War. . . .

Mr. Senator Houston, Hon. Barkley Martin, & several other members of Congress called in the course of the evening, & were greatly excited at the news brought by the Southern mail from the army. They all approved the steps which had been taken by the administration, and were all of opinion that war with Mexico should now be prosecuted with vigor.

PROBLEM 7

# Andrew Johnson:
# Failure in the Presidency

While James K. Polk was able to utilize his resources to become a leader, Andrew Johnson was not. Although some recent biographers might not agree with this harsh judgment, most experts believe that Johnson failed. His policies for the treatment of the South after the Civil War were defeated in Congress. He was impeached by the House of Representatives and almost convicted by the Senate. After serving the remainder of Lincoln's second term, Johnson saw his party pass him by and nominate military hero Ulysses S. Grant for the presidency. Such a record is not one of political skill and leadership.

Why was Johnson not an effective leader? The historian must ask whether Johnson's failure sprang from his personal weaknesses, the nature of the times in which he held office, or some combination of these two factors.

Even Lincoln came from no more humble beginnings than Andrew Johnson. Early orphaned, Johnson did not attend school a day in his life. Apprenticed to a tailor at the age of ten, he was ambitious enough to teach himself to read, and his wife later taught him to write and to do simple arithmetic. He entered the political arena in Tennessee and soon won a reputation as a rough-and-tumble orator who championed the cause of poor whites. Elected to the United States House of Representatives and then to the Senate, Johnson gained much publicity when he became the only southern Senator to support the Union during the Civil War. Lincoln appointed him military governor of Tennessee in 1862, and he served in that post with distinction until he was nominated as Lincoln's running mate in 1864.

When Johnson assumed the presidency, he could have anticipated a successful term, but success would have meant cooperation with the Radicals who wished to see the South humbled. In the first weeks of his administration, Johnson spoke of treason as a crime to be punished, thus leaving the impression that he desired harsh punishment for the South. In reality, however, he believed with Lincoln that the southern states had never legally left the Union and that the reconstruction of these states was clearly a presidential function. This position put him in direct conflict with Radical forces, which he could not control.

Some measure of success can be attributed to Johnson. To his credit, he suffered through the humiliation of his impeachment and trial with great dignity. Through the narrow margin of one vote, Andrew Johnson was spared the disgrace of removal from office on charges which later historians agree were false. The nation was spared what would have amounted to a Congressional dictatorship through a gross miscarriage of justice.

The first reading assesses Johnson's character and traces the breakdown in the relationship between Johnson and Congress over reconstruction policy. The wide gulf between the executive and legislative branches of the government is apparent. The second reading, a newspaper account of Johnson's fiery oratory in 1866, illustrates the volatile temper of the times. The third reading, from the diary of one of Johnson's cabinet members, gives insight into the impeachment trial and Johnson's reactions during that period.

As you read keep the following questions in mind:

**1**　　What were President Johnson's most distinguishing character traits? How did they affect his leadership? Did his experience equip him for the presidency?

**2**　　What was the political situation in which Johnson found himself after Lincoln's assassination? Was Congress favorable to him? What great issues of public policy stirred the electorate?

**3**　　Given the situation, could any President with Johnson's views have succeeded? Did Johnson have particular handicaps?

# I

## THE FIGHT WITH THE RADICALS

In the excerpt which follows, author and Harvard historian Arthur Meier Schlesinger presents a chronological record of the events which led to President Andrew Johnson's impeachment and trial. As has been the case with other elected officials, the effectiveness of Johnson as a political leader was to a great extent dictated by the circumstances of his term in office. Schlesinger considers both the situations which Johnson had to encounter during his presidency and the man's personality. ☐ Arthur Meier Schlesinger, *Political and Social Growth of the American People, 1865–1940*, pp. 10–18. New York: The Macmillan Company, Third Edition copyright © 1941.

The tragic event [Lincoln's death] brought to the White House a man ill fitted by temperament and training to take over the responsibilities at so critical a juncture. Andrew Johnson's rise from humble origins had been even more remarkable than that of Lincoln himself. Starting in poverty and ignorance as a tailor's apprentice, unable to write until taught by his wife, he had fought his way upward by sheer pluck and native ability against tremendous odds and the scorn of the planting aristocracy. When scarcely of age, he was chosen mayor of his little mountain village in eastern Tennessee, an event which proved the first step in a political ascent that took him to the state legislature, the national House of Representatives, the governor's chair and, in 1857, to the United States Senate. Thick-set, swarthy, somber of visage, he had many of Andrew Jackson's mental traits: pugnacity, self-assurance and an immovable loyalty to duty as he conceived it. He stoutly resisted the secession of Tennessee, and his selection as Lincoln's running mate in 1864 was a sop to the War Democrats [who, with the Republicans, favored war to secession] in the party. Long experience in public life wore off some of his rough edges, revealing sterling traits of intellectual courage and inflexible purpose. Unfortunately, the situation before him called also for tact, patience and political skill, and these qualities were utterly foreign to his make-up.

Lincoln's murder put the North in an ugly humor. While the excitement was at fever heat, Johnson offered rewards for the arrest of Jefferson Davis and certain other Southern leaders as accomplices in the terrible deed. Radical chieftains, misled by this passionate action, confidently expected the new President to pursue a vindictive course toward the South, and in their intimate circles they referred to Lincoln's martyrdom as a "godsend to the country." Even the pastor of St. George's

Church in New York told his great congregation, "I do not know but God intended that Lincoln should be removed in order that the proper punishment should be imposed upon the authors of the Rebellion," while Ralph Waldo Emerson, aroused from his philosophic calm in distant Concord, believed that "what remained to be done required new and uncommitted hands."

Johnson disappointed such expectations. As the days passed and his humane instincts rose to the surface again, he adopted the essentials of Lincoln's good-will policy. He announced his acceptance of the Lincoln governments in Virginia, Tennessee, Louisiana and Arkansas, retained his predecessor's cabinet intact, and proceeded to hasten the reconstruction of the remaining states, though insisting on a somewhat wider disfranchisement than Lincoln had required. When the conventions assembled, he made known his wish that they should disavow the ordinances of secession and repudiate their war debts, and that their first legislatures should ratify the pending Thirteenth Amendment. This amendment, proposed by Congress in January, 1865, carried the Emancipation Proclamation to its logical conclusion and precluded the future reëstablishment of slavery. The reorganization of the seven commonwealths [Alabama, Florida, Georgia, Mississippi, North Carolina, South Carolina, Texas] proceeded along these lines, and when Congress gathered on December 4, 1865, for the first time under the new executive, all the states save one [Texas] had substantially complied with the terms. The Thirteenth Amendment was declared a part of the Constitution two weeks later. Texas completed its process of restoration the following April.

The next move now belonged to the legislative branch. Congress, confronted with the question of admitting members from the Southern states, declined to do so. It resented the President's effort to minimize its rôle in reconstruction and, at the same time, it scorned his lenient conditions. In particular, the Radicals censured his failure to require Negro enfranchisement. . . .

The Congress which passed these matters under review contained conservative, moderate and radical Republicans. If Johnson had been prudent enough to conciliate the moderates by slight concessions, he might have preserved the essentials of his plan with the help of the conservatives and of the Democratic minority. But the insolence of the extremists stung him beyond endurance, arousing all his qualities of combativeness and dogmatism. As a result, many of his natural allies were soon driven into league with [Thaddeus] Stevens and [Charles]

Sumner, iron-willed, imperious men who for two years dictated the course of affairs.

The two houses, after setting up a joint committee on reconstruction to formulate Congress's terms for the South, proceeded at once to take action for safeguarding the ex-slaves against the black codes [bills passed by Southern legislatures to control the races socially and economically]. As a first move in this direction, Congress in February, 1866, passed a bill extending the Freedmen's Bureau [a federal agency formed to aid newly freed Negroes and other refugees] indefinitely and enlarging its powers so that it might employ military aid to protect the Negro's rights. The President promptly rejected the bill as an unconstitutional exercise of the war power in time of peace, and in an intemperate speech he classed Stevens and Sumner with Jefferson Davis as traitors to the American system of government. This was Johnson's last victory over Congress. Never again was he able to thwart the will of the opposition. In April Congress adopted over his veto the civil-rights act, which accomplished the purpose of the earlier bill but in a more thorough way. It declared all persons born in the United States (excluding untaxed Indians) to be citizens of the United States and, as such, entitled to the same legal rights as white persons, any "statute . . . to the contrary notwithstanding." Besides inflicting heavy penalties for violations, the statute authorized the use of the troops to secure enforcement. Three months later Congress retrieved its earlier defeat by prolonging the life of the Freedmen's Bureau. . . .

Both Congress and the executive had now indicated their conceptions of a proper reconstruction policy, and the fall elections of 1866 gave the people a chance to choose between them. The President's friends sought to attract the support of the moderates of both political parties, but their promising efforts were unwittingly defeated by Johnson himself when he undertook a "swing round the circle," making a series of blustering extemporaneous speeches in many of the leading cities of the East and Midwest. His cause was further injured by a bloody race riot in New Orleans on July 30, an affray which convinced many Northerners that the South did not intend to deal fairly with the freedmen. Both factions exerted themselves to win the soldier vote by assembling special conventions of the veterans—efforts which may be said to mark the formal entry of the old-soldier influence into postwar politics. In the end, the Radicals won an overwhelming triumph, securing more than two thirds of each branch of Congress. If the President had stayed in Washington, the outcome might have been different. As it was, the Radicals acclaimed the result as a popular mandate to pursue a harsh course toward the South. . . .

The feeling between the President and Congress had grown constantly more vindictive. Johnson vainly vetoed all the important reconstruction measures and, in turn, Congress set about to hamper and defeat his purposes in every conceivable way. One of its efforts, the tenure-of-office act of March 2, 1867, declared the President guilty of a "high misdemeanor" if he removed an officeholder without the Senate's consent. The statute specifically included cabinet officers who, unless the Senate agreed to their dismissal, were to hold office "during the term of the President by whom they may have been appointed and for one month thereafter." Johnson in his ineffectual veto branded the act unconstitutional. Not content with halfway measures, the Radicals determined to depose the President. In their inflamed state of mind, his stubborn resistance to the measures they deemed necessary amounted to disloyalty. The House judiciary committee labored for months to find evidence to justify impeachment on one of the grounds named in the Constitution—"treason, bribery, or other high crimes and misdemeanors"—and in December, by a vote of five to four, reported in favor of such action. But the House decided to await more convincing proof of misconduct.

The opportunity came on February 21, 1868, when Johnson, without consulting the Senate, removed the Secretary of War, Edwin M. Stanton, who had long been acting in secret league with the Radicals. Three days later the House amid intense excitement voted to impeach the President "of high crimes and misdemeanors." The eleven verbose articles of the indictment contained much duplication and confusion of thought, with the principal emphasis placed on Johnson's dismissal of Stanton, which was asserted to constitute a "high misdemeanor" under the tenure-of-office act. The trial in the Senate began on March 30 and lasted until May 26, with Chief Justice Salmon P. Chase presiding. It soon appeared that Johnson had not actually violated the tenure-of-office act, for Stanton, a Lincoln appointee, had continued in service nearly three years after the term of the President who had named him. Nothing daunted, the Radicals turned their efforts toward ousting the chief executive for reasons of party expediency.

The excitement throughout the North was intense, with popular sentiment against Johnson. Even the General Conference of the Methodist Church, then in session at Chicago, set aside an hour of prayer that the Senators might be directed to do their "high duty." When the crucial vote was taken on May 16, the Senate stood 35 to 19 for conviction, one vote short of the necessary two thirds. Seven Republicans defied public opinion to join with the Democratic minority in making this result possible. To posterity it is clear that Johnson had done nothing to merit removal. As Senator Lyman Trumbull said before casting his ballot for acquittal, "Once set the example of impeaching a President for what, when the excitement of the hour shall have subsided, will be regarded as insufficient causes . . . and no future President will be safe who happens to differ with a majority of the House and two thirds of the Senate on any measure deemed by them important."

# II

## JOHNSON TAKES HIS FIGHT TO THE PEOPLE

In the fall of 1866 Johnson made a series of speeches throughout the country to gain support for Congressional candidates favoring a lenient reconstruction policy in the South. The following account of one of his speeches was published on September 3 by the Cleveland *Herald*. ☐ Walter L. Fleming, *Documentary History of Reconstruction*, Volume 1, pp. 220–222. Cleveland, Ohio: The Arthur H. Clark Company, copyright © 1906.

I appear before you to-night and I want to say this: that I have lived and been among all American people, and have represented them in some capacity for the last twenty-five years. And where is the man living, or the woman in the community, that I have wronged, or where is the person that can place their finger upon one single hairbreadth of deviation from one single pledge I have made, or one single violation of the Constitution of our country? What tongue does he speak? What religion does he profess? Let him come forward and place his finger upon one pledge I have violated. [A voice, "Hang Jeff Davis."] [Mr. President resumes.] Hang Jeff Davis? Hang Jeff Davis? Why don't you? [Applause.] Why don't you? [Applause.] Have you not got the court? Have you not got the court? Have you not got the Attorney General? Who is your Chief Justice, and that refused to sit upon the trial? [Applause.] I am not the prosecuting attorney. I am not the jury. But I will tell you what I did do; I called your Congress that is trying to break up the government. [Immense applause.] Yes, did your Congress order hanging Jeff Davis? [Prolonged applause, mingled with hisses].

But, fellow-citizens, we had as well let feelings and prejudices pass; let passion subside; let reason resume her empire. In representing myself to you in the few remarks I intended to make, my intention was to address myself to your judgment and to your good sense, and not to your anger or the malignity of your hearts. This was my object in presenting myself on this occasion, and at the same time to tell you good-bye. I have heard the remark made in this crowd to-night, "Traitor, traitor!" [Prolonged confusion.] My countrymen, will you hear me for my cause? For the Constitution of my country? I want to know when, where and under what circumstances Andrew Johnson, either as Chief Executive, or in any other capacity, ever violated the Constitution of his country. Let me ask this large and intelligent audience here to-night, if your Secretary of State, who served four years under Mr. Lincoln, who was placed under the butcher's blow and exposed to the assassin's knife, when he turned traitor. If I were disposed to play orator, and deal in declamation, here to-night, I would imitate one of the ancient tragedies we have such account of—I would take William H. Seward, and open to you the scars he has received. I would exhibit his bloody garment and show the rent caused by the assassin's knife. [Three cheers for Seward.] Yes, I would unfold his bloody garments here to-night and ask who had committed treason. I would ask why Jeff Davis was not hung? Why don't you hang Thad. Stevens and Wendell Phillips? I can tell you, my countrymen, I have been fighting traitors in the south, [prolonged applause,] and they have been whipped, and say they were wrong, acknowledge their error and accept the terms of the Constitution.

And now as I pass around the circle, having fought traitors at the south, I am prepared to fight traitors at the north, God being willing with your help ["You can't have it," and prolonged confusion] they would be crushed worse than the traitors of the south, and this glorious Union of ours will be preserved. In coming here to-night, it was not coming as Chief Magistrate of twenty-five States, but I come here as the Chief Magistrate of thirty-six States. I came here to-night with the flag of my country in my hand, with a constellation of thirty-six and not twenty-five stars. I came here to-night with the Constitution of my country intact, determined to defend the Constitution let the consequences be what they may. I came here to-night for the Union; the entire circle of these States. [A voice, "How many States made you President?"] How many States made me President? Was you against secession? Do you want to dissolve the Union? [A voice, "No."] Then I am President of the whole United States, and I will tell you one thing. I understand the discordant notes in this audience here to-night. And I will tell you, furthermore, that he that is opposed to the restoration of the government and the Union of the States, is as great a traitor as Jeff. Davis, and I am against both of them. I fought traitors at the south; now I fight them at the north. [Immense applause.]

# III

## THE PRESIDENT ON TRIAL

Gideon Welles, Secretary of the Navy under Lincoln and Johnson, wrote candidly in his *Diary* about the events surrounding Johnson's impeachment and trial. Favoring a lenient reconstruction policy, Welles strongly supported Johnson in his struggle with the Radicals. In the following excerpt, despite his loyalty to the President, he acknowledges Johnson's weaknesses and points to his ineffectiveness in the face of party intrigue. ☐ Gideon Welles, *Diary of Gideon Welles,* Volume 3, pp. 314–315, 319–321. Boston: Houghton Mifflin Company, copyright © 1911.

*March 16, Monday. . . .* It is evident that the Radicals in Congress are in a conspiracy to overthrow not only the President but the government. The impeachment is but a single act in the drama. . . . Should the [Supreme] Court . . . pronounce the Reconstruction laws unconstitutional, the military governments will fall and the whole Radical fabric will tumble with it. Only one course can prolong the miserable contrivance, and that is a President like Wade [Senator from Ohio Benjamin F. Wade, a Radical], who will maintain the military governments regardless of courts, or law, or right. Hence I have very little expectation that the President will escape conviction. His deposition is a party necessity, and the Senators have not individually the strength, ability, nor honesty to resist the Radical caucus decisions which Stevens, Ben Butler, and other chief conspirators sent out.

*March 17, Tuesday.* The Cabinet met in the library, the council room being occupied by the President's lawyers preparing for the impeachment trial. There was little of interest. . . . The President is anxious and more than usually abstracted. I trust he communicates freely with his counsel, though always inclined to be reserved. It has been, and is, his misfortune that he has tried, and still does, to carry on this great government without confidants,—without consulting or advising, except to a very limited extent, with any. It wears upon him, and his measures are not always taken with the caution and care that wisdom dictates.

In his movements the President is irregular. Sometimes he is inexcusably dilatory; sometimes he appears to act from impulse. His best friends expected the removal of Stanton two years earlier than it was made. So far as he communicated anything on the subject, I supposed on several occasions that change would take place. But he delayed until Congress passed a law to prevent Stanton's removal and the President from acting.

The conduct of Stanton was not gratifying to the Radicals, or to one wing of the Republican Party, the more moderate. They were becoming tired of him. A little skillful management would have made a permanent break in that party. But the President had no tact himself to effect it, he consulted with no others, the opportunity passed away, and by a final hasty move, without preparation, without advising with anybody, he took a step which consolidated the Radicals of every stripe, strengthened Stanton, while it weakened his supporters, and brought down a mountain of trouble on himself. Had he unbosomed himself to his Cabinet, received their suggestions, and canvassed fully and deliberately the subject, results would have been different. . . .

*March 23, Monday.* . . . The Radicals are so demoralized and depraved, are so regardless of their constitutional obligations and of their oaths and their duty, that nothing good can be expected of them. But there are unmistakable indications that the Democratic leaders—a set who think more of party than of country—secretly desire the conviction and deposition of the President. Not that they are inimical to him, not that they believe him guilty of any crime deserving of impeachment, not that they will vote against him, but they look upon the act as perfectly suicidal to the Radicals. They [the Democrats] seem not aware that their own unwise conduct is scarcely less suicidal and may save the Radicals from annihilation. . . .

. . . [The] most deplorable, or one of the most deplorable features in all these proceedings is to witness party assemblages, conventions, and legislatures in distant States passing resolutions approving of the impeachment of the President and urging his conviction, without any fact, or specification, or alleged crime, or any knowledge whatever on the subject. Some of these proceedings are sent to Congress and received by the Senate, which sits in judgment. It is not difficult to see the near downfall of a government which shall long pursue a course such as the Radicals are initiating for mere party purposes.

*March 24, Tuesday.* . . . Sumner and certain Senators do not conceal their readiness to proceed at once to judgment and condemnation without proof or testimony. In their unfitness and vindictive partisanship and hate, they would not award the President rights and privileges granted criminals for the court of errors or give him time for preparation. They are really unwilling to allow him to make defense.

These usurpers and conspirators—for they are such, truly and emphatically, having arrogated power without authority, excluded States and people from their constitutional rights of representation—are now deliberately attempting the destruction of another department of the government by the unlawful exercise of these usurped powers. Were all the States represented, as they should be, and would be, if not wickedly and wrongfully excluded by an arbitrary, usurping faction, there could be no conviction, and would have been no impeachment. But the President is arraigned for doing his duty and striving to defend the Constitution in conformity with his oath. The Constitution-breakers are trying the Constitution-defender; the law-breakers are passing condemnation on the law-supporter; the conspirators are sitting in judgment on the man who would not enter into their conspiracy, who was, and is, faithful to his oath, his country, the Union, and the Constitution. What a spectacle! And if successful, what a blow to free government! What a commentary on popular intelligence and public virtue!

# William Marcy Tweed: Political Boss

Men who are responsible for decisions in government command the attention of American newspapers, magazines, radio, and television. While federal, state, and local government officials are focal points of the news, the political manipulators who stand behind the scenes are often almost unknown. However, manipulators perform a vital function in American politics.

People tend to distrust politicians who work behind the scenes. They assume that this kind of man is as corrupt today as in the late nineteenth century, when political bosses controlled many of the large cities. However, manipulators cannot be stereotyped. While many of them have been corrupt, stealing millions from the public purse to line their own pockets, others have been scrupulously honest, seeking only to serve a cause or a party. Some managed to combine personal gain with service to the community.

Manipulators have operated at all levels of American politics and in a variety of ways. Instead of seeking office as a primary goal, they have been content to pull the strings. Some manipulators have never run for office or accepted political appointments. Others have held official positions but exercised their real power through control of patronage and nominations. Unlike political agitators, manipulators usually have avoided the limelight, sacrificing public acclaim for the reality of power.

William Marcy Tweed is the prototype of the big city political boss of the nineteenth century. Born in 1823 in New York City, he was the youngest of five children and his father's favorite. Tweed's father was ambitious for his son's success, and he sacrificed many comforts to send the boy to boarding school. Tweed developed some capability with numbers and kept the books for a tobacco firm. The father's ambitions for his son were further realized when Tweed joined a volunteer fire department. The company competed with other departments in tests of firefighting skill which brought great social prestige and carried little civic responsibility. "Big Bill" Tweed's popularity in the group, combined with his abilities as a showman, carried him to leadership in the fire department and facilitated his entrance into New York City politics. In 1857 he was elected to the Board of Supervisors, which controlled the financial policies of the city, and he helped to expose the corrupt practices of Mayor Fernando Wood. Thus Tweed came to power under the cloak of respectability. Denis Tilden Lynch, in his book *"Boss" Tweed,* cites Tweed's political *credo,* transcribed from testimony at the Aldermanic Committee investigation of the Tweed Ring frauds in 1877:

"The fact is New York politics were always dishonest—long before my [Tweed's] time. There never was a time when you couldn't buy the Board of Aldermen. A politician in coming forward takes things as they are. This population is too hopelessly split up into races and factions to govern it under universal suffrage, except by the bribery of patronage, or corruption."

Although Tweed held positions as New York City alderman, United States Congressman, president of the Board of Supervisors, school commissioner, deputy street commissioner, state senator, and deputy commissioner of public works, he always stood behind the scenes. Nevertheless, by 1870 Tweed, with three allies, controlled the governments of both New York City and New York State.

The excerpts in Problem 8 explore various aspects of Tweed's career. As you read these selections, think about the following questions:

**1**    What were Tweed's goals?

**2**    Who supported Tweed's rise to power? Why?

**3**    What were Tweed's character traits? What particular political skills did he have? Does a political manipulator need character traits and political skills different from those of an agitator? a political theorist?

**4**   How might Readings II and III be biased? Does a political boss perform a necessary function in a democracy?

# I

## THE SOCIAL SETTING OF THE POLITICAL BOSSES

Denis Tilden Lynch states in *"Boss" Tweed,* "Public thieving did not begin with Tweed. Nor did it die with him. It exists because of the apathy of the mass." Oscar Handlin, author of the following excerpt, is well known for his work in American social and economic history. Here, he describes the root of corruption in nineteenth-century city governments, emphasizing the political exploitation of immigrants rather than the "apathy of the mass." □ Oscar Handlin, *The Uprooted,* pp. 210–214. Boston: Little, Brown and Company— Atlantic Monthly Press. Copyright © 1951 by Oscar Handlin. Reprinted by permission.

Throughout the country in the great cities, bosses became the heads of gangs. Some had assembled followings as foremen or contractors, others by growing up in a district where they exercised continuing leadership as a gang of boys grew up to be a gang of voters. Everywhere the connection between these allegiances and the opportunity to work was plain. In an economy that condemned the immigrants to unskilled labor a large percentage of the available jobs were directly or indirectly dependent upon political favor. Aqueducts and streets the city built for itself; trolley, gas, telegraph, and electric lines were laid by companies franchised by the city; and every structure, as it went up, was inspected by the city. One pair of hands was much like another when it held the shovel; the employers of unskilled labor were wise enough to treat indulgently the wishes of the municipal officials in whose power it was to let contracts or grant permits.

The job was at the center of the boss's attractiveness. But he was also able to call forth a more general sense of attachment. Often the feelings of group loyalty focused upon him. He was a member of many associations, made friends on every block. In the columns of their own newspapers his name appeared frequently. His achievements cast their reflected glory on the whole community and he in turn shared its sense of solidarity. In that respect he stood at an advantage over every competitor for the immigrants' leadership. He had sprung from among them and substantially remained one with them.

Furthermore, he spoke for them. After the Civil War as the national parties in election after election chewed over the same stale issues, a great dullness settled down over their campaigns. Few people cared to take the trouble to distinguish how the position of the Democrats differed from that of the Republicans on civil service reform or the tariff. Few even bothered to learn what those problems were about. These were remote and abstract questions that did not directly touch on their own lives. The immigrant might sometimes read an article on such a matter in his newspaper but was less likely to be persuaded by any intrinsic ideas on the subject than by the character of the persuader. If a trusted source said that when a Democrat is President misery comes, that if the Republicans win the factories will open, the new citizen was likely to accept the statement without cavil.

The local issues were the important ones. Whether there should be a new public bathhouse in Ward Twelve, whether the city should hire extra laborers, seemed questions of no moment to the party statesmen. To the residents of the tenement districts they were crucial; and in these matters the ward boss saw eye to eye with them. *Jim gets things done!* They could see the evidence themselves, knew the difference it made in their own existence.

. . . By the century's end, behind the whitened windows of an empty store, in the back room of a saloon, upstairs above the dance hall—under a variety of designations there was in every ward a place where a man could go and see the boss, or see someone who would in turn see the boss.

*I think that there's got to be in every ward a guy that any bloke can go to when he's in trouble and get help—not justice and the law, but help, no matter what he's done.* The old man reminisces as the incidents of a long career come back. What requests had not been made of him! And often enough he'd stepped in without waiting to be asked. Time and again one of the boys would let him know: the poor fellow had allowed his payments to lapse and now the widow had not the burial money; or, the furniture was being put out in the street and them with no place to go and the wife ailing at that. Baskets at Christmas, picnics, boat rides on the river or lake, and a ready purse at the mention of any charitable collection— these were all within his realm of obligations.

But mostly he had intervened at the points at which his people encountered the difficulties of the law. Between the rigid, impersonal rulings of the statute and the human failings of those ignorant of its complexities he stood as mediator. The poor lad who had an extra glass and by some half-remembered encounter ended the night in jail, the shopkeeper whose stand edged beyond the legal limit onto the sidewalk, turned to him whose contact set matters straight. They had all sat there explaining their troubles, the liquor dealer and the peddler worried about licenses, the contractor and the real-estate owner involved in deals with the city. They had come to him because they knew he was *fair* with his favors.

Those vain fools up on the hill had laughed and then seethed with indignation when he had torn the legislature apart so that wretched Italian could vend his peanuts on the grounds. The fulminations against "peanut politics" had been all to the good. They had confirmed the popular impression that he championed the little men against the big, the humble against the proud. Hundreds who themselves never had the occasion to turn to him firmly believed in his accessibility. The image, his own and theirs, was that of the kindly overlord, the feudal noble translated from the manor to the ward—above the law and therefore capable, if properly approached, of doing better justice than the law.

# II

## TWEED'S TACTICS

The Tweed Ring at the height of its power was composed of Tweed and three other men: Mayor A. Oakey Hall, City Comptroller Richard B. Connolly, and City Chamberlain and President of the Board of Parks Peter Barr Sweeny. Tweed served as president of the Board of Supervisors and commissioner of public works. As the leader of the New York City Democratic party machine, Tammany Hall, he was the power behind the elected city government officials. Although the power of the Tweed Ring was broken by 1871, the press continued its investigation of corruption in government. The following selection, published in 1875 in *The North American Review*, describes the operations of the Tweed Ring when it was exercising its greatest influence. □ "An Episode in Municipal Government." Boston: *The North American Review*, Volume 120, January 1875, pp. 127–130.

[Those] who controlled the city government of New York were now supreme at Albany, and William M. Tweed was the master spirit among that little knot of men; in him the Ring was personified. He had now fairly entered upon the full career of success and was at the climax of his glory. His insatiable activity and arrogant self-assertion carried everything before him.

His associates paled into insignificance in the glare of his splendid activity. Sweeny had no desire to rival so boisterous and pushing an ally;

while neither Connolly nor Hall possessed a tithe of his energy. Sweeny and Connolly, moreover, were ever harassed by the fear of exposure, and they protested against Tweed's extravagance and display; he, however, gave a deaf ear to their entreaties and disregarded their warnings.

His influence was supreme, not only in political circles, but with every class of people. A word or note from him was a sure passport to favor. He was as arrogant as he was shameless, and numerous characteristic anecdotes are told of him in both respects, a few of which are worth repeating. One day a henchman of his, who had a place on the police force, being arraigned before the Commissioners for some offence, besought the great man's intercession to save him from dismissal. Tweed, in response to his prayer, went directly to the police headquarters, entered the Commissioners' room, and, demanding the stenographic report of his client's examination, deliberately tore it up and threw it into the waste-paper basket.

He believed every one to be corrupt, and for his own part was guilty of no concealment; in his view all men were either knaves or fools, and the former class admitted of a subdivision between honest knaves and hypocrites. He took pride in being an honest knave, and looked with scornful surprise on a man who, in his own language, gave "sixteen ounces to the pound every time." When [Andrew J.] Garvey, the Court House contractor, was ornamenting his country place at Greenwich, he placed a number of casts of famous pieces of statuary about the grounds. While Tweed was examining the work on its completion, his attention was attracted to these, and he asked what they represented. . . . "Who the h--- is that?" Tweed asked. "That," replied Garvey, "is Mercury, the god of merchants and thieves." "Good! that's bully!" exclaimed Tweed; "put him over the front door." . . .

It does not, of course, need to be said that, with all the splendor of his establishment and equipage, he never arrived at the slightest social recognition; but this he probably regarded as a mere question of time. Neither could he always solace himself with the reflection that his more circumspect neighbors did not scrutinize his money more than that of other people; for once, when unsolicited he sent a contribution of a hundred dollars to the Methodist congregation of Greenwich, which was raising money for the purchase of an altar-cloth, the trustees immediately sent it back to him with a blunt message to the effect that they wanted no stolen money for such an object. Yet that the existence of such a public sentiment need in any way moderate his aspirations never seemed to occur to him. . . .

The temptation to stop and dwell upon the individual traits and peculiarities of so strange a political and moral monstrosity as Tweed is not easy to withstand. It is necessary, however, to recur to the position in which he had now succeeded in establishing himself, and in which he found free scope for the exercise of his avarice as well as for the display of his overbearing nature. Every new financial or industrial enterprise, of whatever nature, in order to be successful, must first set aside a share of its stock to Tweed, and elect him one of its officers. He had but to request a favor for a friend, and it was immediately granted; —for his will was little less than law with every office-holder of the State, from the Governor at Albany to the heads of the different departments in the city.

His daily receptions at the Street Department partook almost of an imperial character. He rapidly and curtly heard complaint and petition, and dismissed each visitor with summary despatch. Besides administering the duties of this office, his attention was also divided among a score of other functions. He was State Senator, chairman of the Democratic State Central Committee, Grand Sachem of Tammany Society, chairman of the General Committee of Tammany Hall, chairman of the Court House Committee, President of the Americus and Blossom Clubs, Director of the Brooklyn Bridge Company, part owner of the New York Printing Company and of the "Transcript" [the official paper of New York City], Director in the Third Avenue and several other Railroad Companies, and President of the Guardian Savings Bank. Well might the "Sun" refer to him as "the multiplied Tweed."

More than once during his earlier life this man had tasted of poverty, and now as he grew older he had no fancy to repeat the experience. He loved money not only for what it would bring,—for he spent lavishly enough,—but he loved it for its own sake. His greed was simply insatiable, and, judging from the published record of the transfers of property, he would seem at one time to have contemplated the purchase of the whole of Manhattan Island. In 1871 he informed a friend that he had just paid off mortgages on his real estate to the extent of two millions of dollars. At another time he boasted that he was already worth twenty millions, and would soon be as rich as Vanderbilt. Indeed, judging by its sudden growth, there is no reason to see why there should have been any limit to his wealth, for at this time he was rapidly and by many and effective processes drawing the whole substance of New York into his own capacious pockets. His hands were everywhere, and wherever they were, they were feeling for money. His proceedings were of every description, but may be said perhaps to have varied from stealing direct to theft consequential. Examples of each phase of peculation [embezzlement] may perhaps as well be described here as elsewhere.

His official position naturally constituted Tweed's base of operations, though scarcely his most fruitful source of profit. As a matter of course he had the Board of Supervisors completely under his control, and met with little difficulty in securing its assent to any schemes, however corrupt. The meetings of this board were held in private and at irregular hours, apparently in order to keep the public in ignorance of its proceedings. A single incident will give a sufficient idea of the high-handed way in which Tweed now ruled it: on one occasion Supervisor Ely made inquiries at the office at 2.30 P.M., on the usual day of meeting, and was informed by the clerk that no meeting was contemplated for that day; at four o'clock on that same day a quorum of the Board was got together by Tweed, and passed the tax levy of about twenty millions, together with a large number of appropriations; they then adjourned without even taking the trouble to notify Mr. Ely that a meeting had been held.

# III

## TWEED AS ROBIN HOOD

In 1870 and 1871 *The New York Times* and *Harper's Weekly* conducted a powerful campaign against Tweed and his henchmen. Earlier attempts at exposing Tweed had failed because newspapers were heavily subsidized by city advertising, and the Ring's money outlasted the reformers' funds. *Times* editor Louis J. Jennings was strengthened in his stand by the support of a bookkeeper who offered proof of corruption in the county auditor's office. The following excerpt is from one of Jennings' editorials. □ "Some Stolen Property Returned," *The New York Times,* Volume 20, Number 6013, December 29, 1870, p. 4.

The other day Mr. Tweed devoted to the "relief of the poor" $50,000, out of the $75,000 which he and Sweeny robbed the public of by means of a single day's *Transcript.* When a man can plunder the public at the rate of $75,000 or $80,000 a day, it does not cost him much of an effort to give a few odd thousand dollars to the "poor." Who, in fact, have done so much as Tweed and his cronies to make people poor? Who has worked so systematically to reduce many a hard-working family to poverty? Having created their destitution, the Tweed gang now contemptuously fling a bone to them to stop their mouths. . . .

The proposal to raise a statue to Mr. Tweed is simply part of the "Christmas mummeries" which the Ring have been carrying on for a week or two past . . . . Let us, if possible, have one of Sweeny to match it, and let them both be flanked by effigies of Moses Taylor and John Jacob Astor [prominent millionaires who investigated Tweed's operations in 1870 and reported that the city government was honest]. It will be a very appropriate gallery of worthies—a collection of New-York's greatest men—and the public will doubtless gaze upon it with affectionate admiration. . . .

. . . If you ask why it is that so many people "stick up" for Tweed and his gang, you have your answer in what is now going on. These rascals know that they *must* share their plunder if they would be kept in their present positions. So they give each other diamond pins and brownstone mansions, and checks for large sums of money and make the public pay all the expenses. Then, by way of cajoling the "working classes," they distribute among them a part of their superfluous riches. Few pause to ask *where* this money originally came from, or how many have been made poorer in order that it might be raised. Bought [bribed] newspapers cry out "how generous" . . . . We live in an age—or at least in a community—which takes men like Tweed and Sweeny, and Connolly and Sands [an opportunist who blackmailed his way into Tweed's operations], and Moses Taylor and John Jacob Astor, and James Fisk, Jr. [a well-known Republican millionaire who surprised people by actively supporting Tweed in 1870], to be types of all that is noble and admirable in our species. It is therefore eminently proper that we should have a statue of Tweed at every street corner. No doubt Washington was removed from the City Hall Park to make room for Tweed—a change which affords a vivid illustration of the two periods in our history represented by the two men. The change has indeed been great. But we still honor something. Men of high character and principle may be at a discount, but we shall never be at a loss for idols while we are content to bend a slavish knee to creatures like Tweed and Fisk, the representatives of all that is basest and vilest in the community.

PROBLEM 9

# Marcus A. Hanna:
# Businessman in Politics

Both Mark Hanna and "Boss" Tweed were political manipulators, yet they played their roles in very different ways. Hanna operated on the national level; Tweed worked in local and state politics. Although both men were rich, Hanna was a successful businessman and Tweed was a grafting politician. Hanna was well educated and moved in the best social circles; Tweed grew up in the streets and never entered New York society.

Hanna worked in a far different political arena from that of Tweed. The latter ran a big city which was beset with problems peculiar to a new urban, industrial society. Tweed's power depended directly on the voters, who seemed to support him and his regime in one election after another. His political strength lay in his skill at organizing voters and manipulating vote tallies. Hanna manipulated a national political party by selecting the men who made the major decisions. His strength depended upon his ability to organize and to persuade influential people. Such a preference for directing the action of other men, rather than deciding issues, gave Hanna and Tweed similar political roles.

Born in 1837 in New Lisbon, Ohio, Hanna moved with his family to Cleveland when he was still in his teens. He became a partner in the family wholesale grocery business but eventually made his fortune in his father-in-law's coal and iron company.

An intelligent and perceptive businessman, Mark Hanna became a successful industrialist and a close friend of Senator William McKinley. Believing that McKinley was the best political leader to uphold the interests of the business community, Hanna began to promote his friend's nomination for the presidency. In 1893 he withdrew from his private affairs to devote himself to that cause. Chosen national chairman of the Republican party in 1896, Hanna managed McKinley's victory over William Jennings Bryan.

Appointed to the Senate in 1897, Hanna served as a United States Senator, while McKinley became the Chief Executive.

The three excerpts in Problem 9 examine Hanna's character and political tactics. As you read, think about the following questions:

**1** What were Hanna's goals? How did he try to reach them?

**2** How did Hanna become a leader? On whom did he depend for support?

**3** What were Hanna's personal attributes? What were his major political skills?

**4** Do you agree with William Allen White that Mark Hanna was not a political boss? Why?

# I

## HANNA'S ROLE IN THE PARTY

William Allen White, editor of the Kansas newspaper *Emporia Daily and Weekly Gazette,* was one of the most astute political observers of his day. The following excerpt is his analysis of Hanna's role in the Republican party during the McKinley administration. ☐ William Allen White, "Hanna." New York: *McClure's Magazine,* Volume 16, Number 1, November 1900, pp. 60, 63–64.

McKinley satisfied something in Hanna. The Canton lawyer was industrious. He was clean. He was reliable. He was ambitious. Hanna's friendship displayed these virtues in the market of public esteem, and held them at their par value. In 1896 Hanna's energy incorporated McKinley, and every business house in the United States, from Wall Street to the carpenter's shop on the alley, took stock. Hanna promoted the candidacy of McKinley before the St. Louis Convention [1896]. He put in that campaign, which ended in the St. Louis Convention, every trained faculty which had made him a successful captain of trade. The outcome was interesting. And American politicians — generally a slipshod lot — who depend much on brass bands and claqueing and flag waving and oratory and beating of tom-toms to swarm their bees, were astounded to see a campaigner use the calculating, exact, business-like methods of a general manager of a railroad. Every Republican Presidential candidate sent out letters by the bushel. Hanna sent McKinley's letters out by the peck. But he picked his correspondents with the care that he picked the officers for his lake ships. It was Hanna's purpose to give the preferred stock in the McKinley syndicate only to men of commercial honor and business standing and political capacity. The whisperer, the Janus-face, the blow-hard, and the promiser were permitted to speculate if they chose, but only upon the general prosperity series. The St. Louis Convention was a meeting of a large board of directors in a business concern. All emotionalism was as remote from the constitution of that body as a sky-rocket from a table of statistics. Hanna had planned the syndicate, he had promoted it, he had made it go. He didn't know who would make the motions, nor who would write up the minutes, nor what phrasing would be used in the prospectus. But he knew the men in the majority, and he knew that they were there to vote for McKinley, and he knew that they were men who accomplish their ends. It was an old story to Hanna — the picking and handling of men. . . .

Hanna is not a boss. The boss in the American political system supplies a human need which the king supplies in other principalities and powers. The people of this Republic expect their boss to rob them, to snub them, to revile them, just as royal subjects expect dishonor and contumely from their king. The parallel runs further; neither a boss nor a king is elected, and it would be as difficult to explain to a republican the divine right of kings as to make a monarchist comprehend the reasons for the domination of the boss. The boss exists outside the actual government of the State; the king is generally extraneous. . . .

. . . Mark Hanna cannot be a boss. First, because a national boss is as impossible to the American people as a national monarch; secondly, Hanna has too well developed a sense of humor to be a boss if he would be. As for the first proposition, a weak popular imagination presumes a weak popular intelligence; and as a nation, the people of this country have more intelligence than is the popular average of intelligence in the boss-ridden cities and States. And as for the second proposition, no living man with a twinkle in his eye and a smile teetering on the threshold of his countenance can view with composure the deadly implacable hunger for a little brief authority which often moves men to sell their souls for it. This hunger is the mainspring which makes the boss a joss [idol]. In politics, he who laughs at the visceral convolutions of the joss is lost. Hanna has to laugh at these things. It is his "nature to"; and when he cannot laugh, he swears, which brings relief to the soul much as laughter does.

Yet in national politics Hanna is a strong man, exceptionally so. He is efficient. He is dominant in his party. Yet in his domination he does not domineer. He accomplishes his end; but not by diplomacy, not by playing man upon man, not like Pontius Pilate, but like Herod. Hanna is a force, not an intrigue. Politics is not his trade; he is a business man first and a politician afterwards; yet he is not a dilettante politician. When he gets in tight places, as in the senatorial election of '97, he does not fight with the foils, but rough and tumble, hand to hand, and with such clubs, dornicks [stones or boulders], and other loose furniture of the environment as the devil may have put in his reach. . . .

The relations existing between Hanna and his friend William McKinley, President of the United States, are particularly interesting. The popular notion of these relations is derived from newspaper cartoons. Probably at least 5,000,000 of the 15,000,000 citizens who will vote at the coming election imagine that Hanna tramps noisily into the White House every morning, gruffly gives his orders for the day's administration to the shivering President, and then walks out and continues to grind the faces off the poor; but the real relations existing between Hanna and McKinley are stranger than fiction. It is McKinley, not Hanna, that controls. The masterful, self-willed, nimble-witted, impetuous, virile Hanna in the presence of the placid, colorless, imperturbable, emotionless, diplomatic, stolid McKinley becomes superficially deferential and considerate of the Presidential dignity, almost to an unnecessary degree. It is known to all men at all familiar with McKinley's administration, that in the differences which have come up in the discussion of administrative affairs, when Hanna has been consulted at all, he has almost invariably yielded his opinion to McKinley's. The friendship—one might call it almost the infatuation of Hanna for McKinley—is inexplicable on any other theory save that of the affinity of opposites. History has often paralleled this affair, but has never fully explained her parallels.

No better evidence may be found to-day that the United States has a representative government than is found in the dominance of Hanna in the majority political party in this nation. Hanna is a representative American. He is the American average. Thomas B. Reed, with his facility for epigram, with his cultured conscience, and with his moral and intellectual courage, stands as far above the American average as Boss Tweed lay below it. Reed is an American ideal; Tweed a horrible example. Mr. Bryan, emotional, fanatic, raw, represents American moments when mob spirit rages; but Hanna, with his apparent faults, which he does not deny, nor his friends try to conceal, and with his undeniable virtues — thrift, industry, practical sense, a cash-register conscience, fidelity, love of truth — with his efficiency — and that covereth a multitude of sins — with his sense of humor, that anchors him to sanity, Hanna is a walking, breathing, living body of the American spirit. It is violating no confidence to announce that certain gentlemen in the Republic — perhaps not a majority of the electorate, but here and there one — do not like to see Mr. Hanna occupying a prominent place in the American government.

Now the remedy for Hannaism — which is the popular name for the civic ailment most bewailed by the gentlemen aforesaid — is not found in lampooning Hanna. Cartoons representing him as a coarse, sordid, brutal hulk of adipose, leading the tin effigy of a President around on wheels, will only convince the youth of the land of one thing: that to be successful in this world one must be coarse, sordid, and brutal — a conviction which the facts in the case of the real Hanna surely belie. The remedy for Hannaism will be found when Hanna's critics give to the exemplification of high civic ideals the force of unqualified success and the charm of virile personality. Until then criticism of Hanna may be esteemed only on account of its literary excellence. For human nature in this perverse generation of vipers admires palpable results rather than impalpable rhetoric.

# II

### LINCOLN STEFFENS ASSESSES HANNA

During the years of Hanna's political influence, *McClure's Magazine* was a popular journal known for its political exposés. As one of *McClure's* outstanding writers, Lincoln Steffens worked to uncover many corrupt practices in city politics. In the following excerpt he evaluates the nature of Mark Hanna's political career. □ Lincoln Steffens, "Ohio: A Tale of Two Cities." New York: *McClure's Magazine*, Volume 25, Number 3, July 1905, pp. 293–296.

The New York *Sun* wondered once how it happened so often that in Ohio men who had spent the better part of their lives in business could step into politics up near the top and prove themselves first-rate politicians from the start. The explanation is simple. Those Ohio men came from Cleveland. If I remember aright, the *Sun* had in mind the sudden appearance of the late Mr. Hanna in national politics with the nomination of Mr. McKinley for president. Mr. Hanna had been in politics for years. Mr. Hanna is one type of the business men who have ruled the City of Cleveland. There are other types, as we shall see, but we must begin with Marcus A. Hanna. He is dead. I don't believe in "nothing but good of the dead;" I believe that true obituaries of our great men would do the living good. But I hoped to be able to tell about Ohio without saying much about Mr. Hanna. That is impossible. You can't understand Cleveland, and you can't understand Ohio, without understanding Mark Hanna. And you can't understand the American people and the United States without seeing Hanna, as he was—good and bad, a delight and a danger, a business man in politics, a business man who dominated a city, became U. S. Senator and the boss of a state, became national head of the dominant national party and was the choice of big business and bad machine politics for President of the United States.

What sort of man was this? He was "our sort." Hanna was American. There are traits American which he lacked, but taken as he stood there was not a fibre of make-up, not a fault, not a virtue, that is not of us. Of Quaker stock from the Virginias, he was born in Ohio's Western reserve [northeast section] and the West made him ripe and rich. Hanna described himself once when in the campaign against Mayor Jones, who was running for governor, he got into a hall full of Welshman. Jones was Welsh, and the crowd jeered at Hanna so that he could not go on with his speech. "There's a lot of American in me," he shouted. "There's some Scotch. Somewheres 'way back, there is Irish blood. But by —, there's no Welsh. If there was, I'd go down there and lick the whole lot of you." That won the Welshmen. They cheered and they listened while Hanna gave Jones and the Welsh fits.

That was Hanna, mixed, but well mixed and, as the politicians say, a "good mixer." He was the fighter who can laugh in his wrath, but won't compromise. "Well, what is your bill?" he was heard to demand of two lobbyists in the Marble Room of the U. S. Senate one day. They murmured some reply. "Well, he don't deserve it, and he don't get it," said Hanna, aloud, and he stumped off to leave them. Then he stopped. "Say, have you — cusses had your lunch? No? Well, I'll give ye a good lunch, but that's all you do get."

Intimate, even familiar, Hanna was always Hanna, in all places, to all men. It is related that at the first inauguration of President McKinley, when he and Hanna rode together from the Capitol to the White House, Mr. McKinley pointed out of the carriage to the Post Office Building and admired it. "Well, that shows how little you know about architecture," said Hanna. . . .

. . . Certainly Hanna was the true type of our successful men of big business. They are men in whom a want is, not like yours, perhaps, or mine, humble, hopeful and capable of dismissal unsatisfied; a want with the Hannas is a lust; no matter how big or how little, no matter how vicious or how innocent, it is Hanna's want; it must be sated and it must be sated now. . . .

Mr. Hanna did not want to go into politics. He had to. It was necessary to his business that he should, and it was for the sake of his business that he did; not for the party, not for the city, not to better things, not even for the sport of it. As a young fellow, he had "batted around" some in his ward for fun; but there was nothing in that for him, so he wasn't regular about it. I inquired closely into this, for I wanted to be sure I wasn't again on a "low down politician's" trail. Mr. Hanna went into politics as a business man, and he always called himself a business-man in politics. . . .

. . . Hanna wasn't a thinker, he was a man of instinct and action, and his unconscious selfishness hurt his effectiveness. The fate of his primitive machine shows that. He did not keep it up regularly. When he wanted something, he worked hard at the organization; when he wanted nothing in particular, he was slack about it. A business man in politics, he ran politics for his business, not for political ends. Some political honors came to him. He went to conventions. He saw how governors were made, and presidents. A delegate to the National Republican Convention of 1888, he was for John Sherman, and he missed a hand in the making of President Harrison. Whether that humble failure suggested it or not, I do not know, but all the world knows that Hanna came to have a great ambition that was political. He wanted to have a president. He chose William McKinley, and he planned for years his nomination in 1896. That he succeeded, everybody knows. Hanna often laughed, in his merry way, at the "spontaneous demand" for McKinley, which swept over the country at just the right time. Hanna organized that demand. He dotted the country with men primed to shout at a signal and when he gave the word, the wave rose and rolled in upon the convention where Hanna was dickering for its enthusiastic reception.

And Hanna won with McKinley and money, Hanna and the System — in the United States.

# III

## HANNA AND THEODORE ROOSEVELT

It was generally known by political insiders that Mark Hanna had little respect for the stormy Theodore Roosevelt. He advised McKinley against accepting "the cowboy" as a vice-presidential running mate in 1900. Herman Henry Kohlsaat, a Chicago businessman and newspaper publisher, was a personal friend of many Presidents, including McKinley and Roosevelt. In the following reading, he tells how Hanna was brought around to accepting and working with Roosevelt after McKinley's assassination. □ Herman Henry Kohlsaat, *From McKinley to Harding,* pp. 100–103. New York: Charles Scribner's Sons, copyright © 1923.

Roosevelt occupied a drawing-room. He asked me [Kohlsaat] to sit with him. His mind was working like a trip-hammer. He talked of many things he was going to do.

Part of the time I was in the second Pullman. An hour or two after leaving Buffalo Mark Hanna came to my seat. He was in an intensely bitter state of mind. He damned Roosevelt and said: "I told William McKinley it was a mistake to nominate that wild man at Philadelphia. I asked him if he realized what would happen if he should die. Now look, that damned cowboy is President of the United States!"

I tried to reason with him; told him Roosevelt did not want to be "shot into the Presidency," but could not mollify him.

A little later I asked Roosevelt how he and Mark Hanna got along. He said: "Hanna treats me like a boy. He calls me 'Teddy.'" I asked him if he realized what it meant if he and Hanna quarrelled, and told him Hanna held the Republican organization in the hollow of his hand; that he was the leader in the Senate and could defeat any measure that he, Roosevelt, proposed, and make his administration a failure. . . .

Roosevelt said: "What can I do about it? Give him complete control of the patronage!" I said: "Hanna would resent any such suggestion." I told him Hanna was heart-broken. He saw his best friend gone. All his hopes crushed.

Finally I made the suggestion he invite Hanna to take supper with him alone in his drawing-room. That he must not say anything in the presence of the waiter that could be repeated, as the newspaper men would pounce upon the poor colored boy when they arrived in Washington. That after the plates and cloth were removed, to let the table remain, calling his attention to the awful gap between the front and back seat of a Pullman sleeper. When they were alone, to say: "'Old man, I want you to be my friend. I know you cannot give me the love and affection you gave McKinley, but I want you to give me just as much as you can. I need you. Will you be my friend?' Then put your hands, palms up, on the table. If he puts his hands in his pockets, you are a goner, but if he puts his hands in yours, you can bet on him for life." Roosevelt said: "All right, I'll try it!"

Later, as I sat in the forward coach, I saw the waiter whisper in Senator Hanna's ear. He hesitated a moment, and then nodded his head. He came to my seat at the other end of the car and said: "That damned cowboy wants me to take supper with him, alone. Damn him!" I said: "Mark, you are acting like a child. Go and meet him half-way."

Shortly after, he disappeared into Roosevelt's car. I was very nervous, but as an hour passed and thirty minutes more, Hanna came in, and I knew by his face, as he limped toward my seat, it was "all right." With a smile which . . . "would grease a wagon," Hanna said: "He's a pretty good little cuss, after all!" When I asked him what took place, he told me of Roosevelt's putting his hands on the table, and as near as one man can quote another, he told what Roosevelt said, repeating what I had told Roosevelt to say. "What did you do, Mark?" He answered: "Putting my hands in his I said: 'I will be your friend on two conditions: first, that you carry out McKinley's policies, as you promised.' Roosevelt answered: 'All right, I will.' 'Second, that you quit calling me "old man."' If you don't, I'll call you "Teddy."' ' 'All right. You call me "Teddy" and I'll call you "old man."' '" From that moment Roosevelt and Hanna were stanch, loyal friends. The only rift was for a few weeks late in 1903, when some anti-Roosevelt people tried to get Mark Hanna into the race for the Presidency.

All of Roosevelt's own writings and his numerous biographies tell of his friendly relations with Hanna, but are silent as to how it came about.

# Eugene Victor Debs:
## Socialist

Eugene V. Debs was, like Samuel Adams, an agitator who worked to replace one political system with another. Adams succeeded; as much as any other man, he helped bring about the American Revolution. Debs failed in his attempt to replace American capitalism with socialism.

Debs was a labor leader and a socialist. As did many agitators who shared his interest in these causes, Eugene Debs viewed the established upper class as the enemy of the working class. The Socialist party that Debs led never became more than a minor power in United States politics, yet many of the principles which he held and even some of the programs he supported have been accepted by millions of voters, representing both the working class and the upper class.

An idealist, completely devoted to his principles, Eugene Debs preferred a prison sentence to compromise. Over and over again, he risked his life for causes in which he believed. Consumed by his beliefs, Debs found little meaning in material success or personal acclaim, and his untiring zeal attracted many followers. More than 900,000 voters endorsed his last presidential candidacy in 1920, a campaign which Debs conducted while in prison.

Born in 1855 in Terre Haute, Indiana, Debs went to work in the shops of the Terre Haute and Indianapolis Railway at the age of fifteen. In 1893 he helped organize the American Railway Union and was chosen its president. Arrested and jailed for his role in organizing the Pullman strike in 1894, Debs read socialist literature while in prison. He became an ardent Socialist and ran five times as the party candidate for President. Because Debs was a pacifist, he actively opposed American intervention in World War I. He was arrested under the 1917 Espionage Act, tried, and sentenced to prison in 1918. President Harding pardoned him in 1921, five years before his death.

Problem 10 consists of three excerpts. In the first, Debs describes his path from railway worker to socialist agitator. The second, one of his editorials, gives insights into some of the techniques he used to arouse public opinion. The final excerpt, an obituary from *The Nation,* assesses Debs' character and his contribution to American life.

As you read, think about the following questions:

**1**    What were Debs' goals and how did they change? How did Debs hope to reach his goals?

**2**    What were Debs' outstanding political skills? What does the choice of words in the first two readings reveal about his skills? How were his skills suited to his role as an agitator?

**3**    Compare Debs' methods as a labor leader and as a political agitator. Did he operate from within or from outside of the formal political structure?

**4**    Do you agree or disagree with the editorial comment on Debs in Reading III? How else might you evaluate the man and his work? Why?

# I

## HOW DEBS BECAME A SOCIALIST

Debs wrote the following account of his conversion to socialism for a party magazine, *The Comrade.* When the article was first published in April 1902, Debs prefaced it with this explanation: "As I have some doubt about the readers of *The Comrade* having any curiosity as to 'how I became a Socialist' it may be in order to say that the subject is the editor's not my own; and that what is here offered is at his bidding—my only concern being that he shall not have cause to wish that I had remained what I was instead of becoming a Socialist." □ Eugene V. Debs, *Writings and Speeches of Eugene V. Debs,* pp. 43–47. New York: Hermitage Press, Inc., copyright © 1948.

On the evening of February 27, 1875, the local lodge of the Brotherhood of Locomotive Firemen was organized at Terre Haute, Ind., by Joshua A. Leach, then grand master, and I was admitted as a charter member and at once chosen secretary. "Old Josh Leach," as he was affectionately called, a typical locomotive fireman of his day, was the founder of the brotherhood, and I was instantly attracted by his rugged honesty, simple manner and homely speech. How well I remember feeling his large, rough hand on my shoulder, the kindly eye of an elder brother searching my own as he gently said, "My boy, you're a little young, but I believe you're in earnest and will make your mark in the brotherhood." Of course, I assured him that I would do my best. What he really thought at the time flattered my boyish vanity not a little when I heard of it. He was attending a meeting at St. Louis some months later, and in the course of his remarks said: "I put a tow-headed boy in the brotherhood at Terre Haute not long ago, and some day he will be at the head of it." . . .

At the convention held in Buffalo in 1878 I was chosen associate editor of the magazine, and in 1880 I became grand secretary and treasurer. With all the fire of youth I entered upon the crusade which seemed to fairly glitter with possibilities. For eighteen hours at a stretch I was glued to my desk reeling off the answers to my many correspondents. Day and night were one. Sleep was time wasted and often, when all oblivious of her presence in the still small hours my mother's hand turned off the light, I went to bed under protest. Oh, what days! And what quenchless zeal and consuming vanity! . . .

My grip was always packed; and I was darting in all directions. To tramp through a railroad yard in the rain, snow or sleet half the night, or till daybreak, to be ordered out of the roundhouse for being an "agitator," or put off a train, sometimes passenger, more often freight, while attempting to deadhead over the division, were all in the program, and served to whet the appetite to conquer. . . .

I rode on the engines over mountain and plain, slept in the cabooses and bunks, and was fed from their pails by the swarthy stokers who still nestle close to my heart, and will until it is cold and still.

Through all these years I was nourished at Fountain Proletaire. I drank deeply of its waters and every particle of my tissue became saturated with the spirit of the working class. I had fired an engine and been stung by the exposure and hardship of the rail. I was with the boys in their weary watches, at the broken engine's side and often helped to bear their bruised and bleeding bodies back to wife and child again. How could I but feel the burden of their wrongs? How could the seed of agitation fail to take deep root in my heart?

And so I was spurred on in the work of organizing, not the firemen merely, but the brakemen, switchmen, telegraphers, shopmen, track-hands, all of them in fact, and as I had now become known as an organizer, the calls came from all sides and there are but few trades I have not helped to organize and less still in whose strikes I have not at some time had a hand.

In 1894 the American Railway Union [A. R. U.] was . . . [mobilized for the Pullman strike] and a braver body of men never fought the battle of the working class.

Up to this time I had heard but little of Socialism, knew practically nothing about the movement, and what little I did know was not calculated to impress me in its favor. I was bent on thorough and complete organization of the railroad men and ultimately the whole working class, and all my time and energy were given to that end. My supreme conviction was that if they were only organized in every branch of the service and all acted together in concert they could redress their wrongs and regulate the conditions of their employment. The stockholders of the corporation acted as one, why not the men? It was such a plain proposition — simply to follow the example set before their eyes by their masters—surely they could not fail to see it, act as one and solve the problem. . . .

The skirmish lines of the A. R. U. were well advanced. A series of small battles was fought and won without the loss of a man. A number of concessions was made by the corporations rather than risk an encounter. Then came the fight on the Great Northern, short, sharp, and decisive. The victory was complete — the only railroad strike of magnitude ever won by an organization in America.

Next followed the final shock — the Pullman strike — and the American Railway Union again won, clear and complete. The combined corporations were paralyzed and helpless. At this juncture there was delivered, from wholly unexpected quarters, a swift succession of blows that blinded me for an instant and then opened wide my eyes — and in the gleam of every bayonet and the flash of every rifle *the class struggle was revealed.* This was my first practical lesson in Socialism, though wholly unaware that it was called by that name.

An army of detectives, thugs and murderers was equipped with badge and beer and bludgeon and turned loose; old hulks of cars were fired; the alarm bells tolled; the people were terrified; the most startling rumors were set afloat; the press volleyed and thundered, and over all the wires sped the news that Chicago's white throat was in the clutch of a red mob; injunctions flew thick and fast, arrests followed, and our office and headquarters, the heart of the strike, was sacked, torn out and nailed up by the "lawful" authorities of the federal government; and . . . in company with my loyal comrades I found myself in Cook County jail at Chicago with the whole press screaming conspiracy, treason and murder . . . .

The Chicago jail sentences were followed by six months at Woodstock [Illinois jail] and it was here that Socialism gradually laid hold of me in its own irresistible fashion. Books and pamphlets and letters from Socialists came by every mail and I began to read and think and dissect the anatomy of the system in which workingmen, however organized, could be shattered and battered and splintered at a single stroke. . . .

It was at this time, when the first glimmerings of Socialism were beginning to penetrate, that Victor L. Berger [Socialist Congressman from Wisconsin] — and I have loved him ever since — came to Woodstock, as if a providential instrument, and delivered the first impassioned message of Socialism I had ever heard — the very first to set the "wires humming in my system." As a souvenir of that visit there is in my library a volume of "Capital" by Karl Marx, inscribed with the compliments of Victor L. Berger, which I cherish as a token of priceless value.

The American Railway Union was defeated but not conquered — overwhelmed but not destroyed. It lives and pulsates in the Socialist movement, and its defeat but blazed the way to economic freedom and hastened the dawn of human brotherhood.

# II

## "AROUSE, YE SLAVES"

The following excerpt is Debs' defense of two officials of the Western Federation of Miners, W. D. ("Big Bill") Haywood and Charles Moyer, who had been accused of instigating the assassination of Idaho Governor Frank Steunenberg in 1905. Haywood's and Moyer's accusers were anti-union men, and, in defending labor union officials, Debs defended the right of men to organize into unions. In the same speech he strongly denounced capitalism in general. The Appeal to Reason published free-lance socialist periodicals. □ Eugene V. Debs, *Debs: His Life, Writings and Speeches*, pp. 309–311. Girard, Kansas: The Appeal to Reason, copyright © 1908.

The latest and boldest stroke of the plutocracy, but for the blindness of the people, would have startled the nation.

Murder has been plotted and is about to be executed in the name and under the forms of law.

Men who will not yield to corruption and browbeating must be ambushed, spirited away and murdered.

That is the edict of the Mine Owners' Association [an organization opposed to the formation of unions] of the western states and their Standard Oil backers and pals in Wall street, New York.

These gory-beaked vultures are to pluck out the heart of resistance to their tyranny and robbery, that labor may be left stark naked at their mercy.

Charles Moyer and Wm. D. Haywood, of the Western Federation of Miners, and their official colleagues—men, all of them, and every inch of them—are charged with the assassination of ex-Governor Frank Steunenberg, of Idaho, who simply reaped what he had sown, as a mere subterfuge to pounce upon them in secret, rush them out of the state by special train, under heavy guard, clap them into the penitentiary, convict them upon the purchased perjured testimony of villains, and strangle them to death with the hangman's noose.

It is a foul plot; a damnable conspiracy; a hellish outrage. . . .

Moyer, Haywood and their comrades had no more to do with the assassination of Steunenberg than I had; the charge is a ghastly lie, a criminal calumny, and is only an excuse to murder men who are too rigidly honest to betray their trust and too courageous to succumb to threat and intimidation.

Labor leaders that cringe before the plutocracy and do its bidding are apotheosized; those that refuse must be foully murdered.

Personally and intimately do I know Moyer, Haywood, . . . and their official co-workers, and I will stake my life on their honor and integrity; and that is precisely the crime for which, according to the words of the slimy "sleuth" who "worked up the case" against them, "they shall never leave Idaho alive." . . .

Nearly twenty years ago the capitalist tyrants put some innocent men to death for standing up for labor. [As a result of the Haymarket Riot in 1886, eight men were tried and found guilty of inciting the disturbance. Four of them were executed.]

They are now going to try it again. Let them dare!

There have been twenty years of revolutionary education, agitation and organization since the Haymarket tragedy, and if an attempt is made to repeat it, there will be a revolution and I will do all in my power to precipitate it.

The crisis has come and we have got to meet it. Upon the issue involved the whole body of organized labor can unite and every enemy of plutocracy will join us. From the farms, the factories and stores will pour the workers to meet the red-handed destroyers of freedom, the murderers of innocent men and the arch-enemies of the people.

Moyer and Haywood are our comrades, staunch and true, and if we do not stand by them to the shedding of the last drop of blood in our veins, we are disgraced forever and deserve the fate of cringing cowards.

We are not responsible for the issue. It is not of our seeking. It has been forced upon us; and for the very reason that we deprecate violence and abhor bloodshed we cannot desert our comrades and allow them to be put to death. If they can be murdered without cause so can we, and so will we be dealt with at the pleasure of these tyrants.

They have driven us to the wall and now let us rally our forces and face them and fight.

If they attempt to murder Moyer, Haywood and their brothers, a million revolutionists, at least, will meet them with guns.

They have done their best and their worst to crush and enslave us. Their politicians have betrayed us, their courts have thrown us into jail without trial and their soldiers have shot our comrades dead in their tracks.

The worm turns at last, and so does the worker.

Let them dare to execute their devilish plot and every state in the Union will resound with the tramp of revolution.

Get ready, comrades, for action! No other course is left to the working class. Their courts are closed to us except to pronounce our doom. To enter their courts is simply to be mulcted of our meager means and bound hand and foot; to have our eyes plucked out by the vultures that fatten upon our misery.

Whatever is done we must do ourselves, and if we stand up like men from the Atlantic to the Pacific and from Canada to the Gulf, we will strike terror to their cowardly hearts and they will be but too eager to relax their grip upon our throats and beat a swift retreat.

A special revolutionary convention of the proletariat at Chicago, or some other central point, would be in order, and, if extreme measures are required, a general strike could be ordered and industry paralyzed as a preliminary to a general uprising.

If the plutocrats begin the program, we will end it.

# III

## A EULOGY

The following editorial was written as a eulogy to Eugene Debs. ☐ "Eugene Victor Debs." New York: *The Nation,* Volume 123, Number 3200, November 3, 1926, p. 443.

"'Gene Debs was the only Jesus Christ I ever knew." So Sam Moore, an embittered Negro convict faced with lifelong imprisonment, explained to the warden of Atlanta Penitentiary the extraordinary effect upon him of 'Gene Debs's friendship. 'Gene Debs was a man who evoked that extravagant, almost unbelievable, type of affection in thousands upon thousands of his fellow-men. He evoked it because he gave it. At his funeral services in Terre Haute Victor Berger said that Debs went beyond the Biblical command to love thy neighbor as thyself, for he loved his neighbor better than himself, and the vast crowd with tear-stained faces solemnly nodded assent.

To this love for human beings Debs added a love for humanity. The two are not always combined. The concern for humanity, the vision, the dauntless courage, the uncompromising spirit of the prophet and pioneer may be consistent with a ruthless disregard for the immediate interests of individual human beings. It was not so with Debs. His courage was born of love. His passion for mankind, his hope for the workers grew out of the love of comrades, not only as they might become but as they were with all their faults and weaknesses. In this combination of dauntless prophet, far-seeing idealist, and simple lover of men lay the man's greatness.

Debs embraced the cause of the workers from choice and not necessity. The outward circumstances of his early life and his own gifts were of a sort that would have led him naturally to political and financial success. Indeed, while he was still a very young man, he made a successful beginning in local politics. But his sympathies, long before he was a Socialist, were with the workers. Our generation has almost forgotten that Debs began as an unusually successful labor organizer. He was the founder of the present Brotherhood of Railway Trainmen. When he became convinced that this form of craft organization was not adequate to the needs of the railway workers he resigned his $4,000-a-year position to become president of the American Railway Union at $900 a year. The world still remembers that union and its part in the Pullman strike.

The strike and the union were both broken by Grover Cleveland's use of United States troops against the protest of Governor [John P.] Altgeld of Illinois. This strike, too, was marked by the beginning of government by injunction, and Debs was sent to jail for six months on a charge of contempt—the forerunner of a series of similar acts of judicial tyranny.

In prison Debs first learned of Socialism and became a Socialist, although not until after the first [William Jennings] Bryan [presidential] campaign [in 1896] did he irrevocably tie his fortunes to that movement. Following his release from prison Debs undertook to raise and pay off $40,000 of debts accumulated by the American Railway Union. This obligation he fulfilled at great cost to himself at a time when not even the creditors of the union held him responsible.

From 1897 on, Debs's life and fortunes were inextricably mingled with those of the Socialist movement. Five times he was its candidate for President. He was not primarily a builder of policies, nor in his later years an organizer. He was a flaming spirit, a living incarnation of an ideal. That ideal was an ideal of uncompromising struggle, but of struggle by non-violent methods. The victory he wanted was a victory of peace. It was impossible that Debs could believe the European war a war for democracy, or that any war could end war. So he made himself the spokesman of the Socialist ideal of peace through an understanding between the workers of the world. For his devotion to liberty and peace he was sentenced to ten years of penal servitude. Today it seems almost unthinkable that on the basis of his famous . . . speech [at Canton, Ohio, on June 16, 1918] any man could have been convicted. In no sense were his words pro-German. They did not ask American troops to lay down their arms. They were a plea for the end of war, for the recognition of Russia, for the preservation of liberty at home. Yet that speech, during a "war for democracy," sent a man past sixty years of age, suffering from the heart disease which finally resulted in his death, to jail with common felons. Worse still, after the armistice Debs was kept in jail by the personal vindictiveness of a President who had himself acknowledged the economic causes of the war as plainly as the man whom he held prisoner. It was left to President Harding, in response to public demand, to restore Debs to freedom. Neither he nor President Coolidge gave him back his citizenship.

Of Debs's permanent place in the history of the labor movement and of social progress it is too early to speak. Philosophically, in spite of the Communist attempt to claim him, he was an extreme democrat, a convinced believer in freedom. However much he might admire the achievements of Russia, he never could identify himself with any sort of dictatorship. Our generation with its little faith in the common man may find his philosophy old-fashioned. Temporarily, at least, it has lost much of its appeal. Yet Debs himself was the sort of man who gives one new confidence in men and their possibilities. That he was what he was, that he loved as he loved, is reason for hope. He belongs to the republic of the immortals whose memory is a living inspiration to mankind.

PROBLEM 11

# Joseph G. Cannon: Autocrat of the House

Joseph Gurney Cannon served in the United States House of Representatives for forty-six years and reigned as Speaker from 1903 to 1910. The power that he exercised while he ruled provoked great controversy in the House and throughout the nation.

Within the legislative framework of the federal government, Congressional decision-makers follow informal rules, sometimes called folkways, as well as more formal procedures. By custom, for example, freshman Senators seldom speak from the floor of the chamber. If this folkway is violated, the older members of the Senate may resent the new legislator and show him little cooperation. The formal rules established by the House of Representatives and the Senate are even more important. Within each chamber, these formal rules establish a hierarchy of authority, necessary to the efficient functioning of the legislative process. Holding a position of power under these rules, a man may exert enormous influence on the course of legislation. Moreover, a stubborn and confident man in such a position can frustrate the wishes of an entire nation.

The House of Representatives has been the scene of many historic debates and has furnished a stage for many American political personalities. Not the least significant of these debates was the one which centered about the power exercised by Speaker Joseph G. Cannon. "Uncle Joe," as he was familiarly known to many people, had first entered the House in 1873 as Republican Representative from the Danville district in Illinois. Cannon was known for his honesty and integrity. Self-assured and stubborn, he was unyielding in the face of argument.

When Cannon was elected Speaker of the House, he began a reign of arbitrary rule which came to be known as "Cannonism." His power was based on a House rule which gave him full authority to appoint all the members of House committees. By 1907 signs of revolt began to appear when members who dared oppose "Uncle Joe" were purged from the most desirable committee assignments. When the 61st Congress opened in March of 1909, Champ Clark, Democratic Representative from Missouri, led an unsuccessful attempt to restrict the power of the Speaker. Not until March 1910 did a coalition of Democrats and insurgent Republicans succeed in reducing the Speaker's power. The important Committee on Rules, which decided what legislation would be considered, was expanded and its membership was no longer to be appointed by the Speaker, but by vote of House members. The Speaker was removed from this committee, of which he had formerly been Chairman.

As you read, keep the following questions in mind:

**1** What seem to have been Cannon's aims? What was his position in the House of Representatives? How was he able to use this position to achieve his objectives?

**2** Were Cannon's aims selfish? Who gained by his methods? Who lost?

**3** Why were the House rules changed? How was leadership divided over the issue of changing the rules? What were the results of these changes?

**4** What does this incident reveal about the institutional setting of leadership in American politics? How were personal power and the organization of the House of Representatives related in this instance?

# I

## BREAKING CANNON'S POWER

George Norris, Republican Representative from Nebraska, led the House of Representatives in the widely publicized fight to break the power of Speaker

Joseph G. Cannon. The "Insurgent revolt" divided the Republican members of the House into the Insurgents and the regular Republicans. Joined by their Democratic colleagues, the Insurgents destroyed Cannon's autocratic control of the House. The following editorial is an account of that revolt. □ Ernest Hamlin Abbott, "The Liberation of the House." New York: *The Outlook*, April 2, 1910, pp. 750–752.

When scores of men of varying political beliefs and of conflicting interests assemble to enact laws, they at once face the necessity of adopting some methods for doing business and compromising minor differences. If only a few members of the assemblage propose legislation, and the bills they introduce are not numerous or complicated, the problem is comparatively simple. All that they need to do is to select some one to preside and see that business is taken up in some kind of orderly fashion. When, however, the members propose a multitude of measures, many of them involving matters of little moment, and others great policies of government, and some of them intricate and technical, the problem becomes serious.

In the first Congress there were less than two hundred bills introduced; in the last Congress [the 61st] there were nearly forty thousand. In the first Congress the legislation concerned a people whose problems were comparatively simple; in the last Congress it concerned ninety millions of heterogeneous people living under a most complicated industrial and social system.

In any circumstances, even with only two hundred bills to consider, there must be some way by which the assemblage may decide what measures are most important. In England the Cabinet, the responsible Ministry, virtually decides. In this country the Cabinet is purely executive; there is no Ministry responsible for legislation. So the work of deciding what measures are of most importance is apportioned among all the members of the House. The House is divided up into committees, each charged with the care of one class of legislation. These committees take the bills that are introduced and sort them, throwing some aside and reporting others to the whole House, with their recommendations. Even after this sorting the mass of legislation is large. A small group of men opposed to a particular measure could . . . frustrate the will of the majority. Various plans have been adopted to prevent this. Among them is the creation of a Committee on Rules, which can select measures to receive attention.

These committees, including the Committee on Rules, are supposed to be selected by the majority of the members of the House. Now, since the majority chooses the Speaker, it was decided (in 1790) that the Speaker, representing the majority, should choose the committees. Among other committees, he has heretofore chosen the Committee on Rules, and has been a member and Chairman of it. A child can see that a Speaker can very largely determine what bills shall or shall not be passed, not only by designating members to committees, but especially by his appointments to the Committee on Rules and his own membership in that Committee. Again and again, from 1804 on, the attempt has been made to take from the Speaker the power to appoint committees. Each time it has failed.

Against other powers assumed by the Speaker there has been on various occasions vigorous, sometimes violent, protest; but still, because of the need for guarding against obstruction, these powers have been allowed to accumulate.

At last Joseph G. Cannon was elected Speaker. Skilled in parliamentary law, astute in making adjustments between conflicting interests, inexorable in punishing recalcitrant members, he used these powers to mold legislation not merely to promote his party's policies, but to promote his own views of those policies.

Then the protest became a movement. Republicans who felt that their own Speaker was using the powers of his office unfairly came out into the open as insurgents against Mr. Cannon and his lieutenants. With the aid of Democratic votes, however, the majority of the Republicans last year re-elected Mr. Cannon Speaker. "Cannonism" became an issue. It was thus partly a personal issue and partly an issue of principle. Some of the Insurgents were offended because of Mr. Cannon's treatment of them; some desired legislation which they believed Mr. Cannon was blocking, or opposed legislation which they thought he was promoting; some were fighting against the practice of trading and bargaining between private interests, which Mr. Cannon avowedly followed, and wished to have the right to legislate for the public interest; but all agreed that no one man should have the power exercised by Mr. Cannon, and that the House should be liberated. On the other hand, Mr. Cannon repeatedly said that the majority could depose the Speaker and change the rules; and that his remaining in power showed that the majority approved of his conduct. . . .

Some time ago, Mr. Norris, an Insurgent from Nebraska, had prepared a resolution taking from the Speaker not only the chairmanship and even membership on the Committee on Rules, but also his power to appoint the Committee, giving that power to the House instead. He had been waiting for a chance to present his resolution; but he did not find it. The Speaker's power to recognize or not recognize members on the floor, the prearrangement of business, the whole system of the House, stood in the way.

Finally, one day, a fellow-member, Mr. [Edgar Dean] Crumpacker [Republican from Indiana], rose and presented a resolution regarding census legislation. After a disagreement between the Speaker and the House, in which the Speaker was on two successive days defeated, Mr. Crumpacker's resolution was declared in order because the Constitution said that the House should take a census.

Thereupon Mr. Norris proposed his resolution, and declared it to be in order because the Constitution authorized the House to make its own rules. Immediately there was great excitement. The Speaker's power was threatened.

Since the regular Republicans had been defeated by the combined votes of the Democrats and Insurgents on the Crumpacker resolution, they foresaw defeat again. Resorting to dilatory tactics, which are the usual resource of a minority, these regular Republicans, the majority of the majority, used the passing time to get voters to sustain the Speaker. All night the advocates and opponents of the resolution debated. And the Speaker, awaiting reinforcements, refused to rule whether it was in order or not. When Friday, the 18th of March, dawned, the House was still in session.

Meantime a committee of the Insurgents met with a committee of the Regulars and offered a compromise, but all to no purpose. Neither explicitly nor by informal but binding agreement would the Regulars consent to any plan which would take the Speaker off the Committee on Rules.

So Friday passed, and the House took a recess. Reconvening on Saturday, the House heard for the first time the ruling of the Speaker that the Norris resolution was not in order. He cited a precedent to show that the right of the House to make its own rules was not equivalent to a Constitutional right to amend the rules at any time.

Mr. Norris appealed to the judgment of the House. Mr. [John] Dalzell [Republican from Pennsylvania] then moved to lay Mr. Norris's appeal on the table. If Mr. Dalzell's motion had prevailed, it would have meant the retention of the Speaker's power. The roll was called and the motion was lost. The Democrats, in an unbroken body, and the compact group of Insurgents showed that they could outvote the forces of Speaker Cannon.

Then, after a vote ordering the previous question, Mr. Norris's appeal was sustained. That established as a precedent the principle that the House may at any time amend its rules. Next, in a form changed as to details, the new rule was adopted. This eliminated the Speaker from the Rules Committee, which was enlarged from five to ten members, and transferred from the Speaker to the House the power of appointing the Committee itself.

# II

## A CONGRESSMAN ANALYZES "CANNONISM"

Representative Victor Murdock of Kansas was an Insurgent. The following reading is Murdock's account of what the defeat of Cannonism meant to representative government. ☐ Victor Murdock, "After Cannonism—What?" New York: *The Independent,* Volume 69, Number 3225, September 22, 1910, pp. 622–625.

Take away from the office of Speaker the power to appoint committees — there can be no complete victory over Cannonism without that. In this power is the greatest source of the outrageous control of the House by its presiding officer. The war waged against Cannon must be continued to prevent a return of Cannonism under any future Speaker, whatever his political party.

For it is of the utmost importance that the American people, having defined the evil of Cannonism, and having determined upon its punishment, should proceed to plug up the drain which has been poisoning representative government. To this end the people should demand that the House itself, and not the Speaker, appoint the committees.

When the House insurgents arose, two years ago, most of them, uncertain of popular support, insisted that they had no attack upon Mr. Cannon; that their effort for correction was confined to the system of legislative procedure. The people themselves, once the attack opened, did not limit their impeachment to impersonal Cannonism. On the contrary, popular attack concentrated almost wholly on Cannon, the man. It would be a grievous mistake for the nation to believe that the trouble was wholly Cannon or wholly Cannonism. The trouble was both. The thing now to consider is that Cannonism does not necessarily pass with the retirement of Cannon. The one certain way to see that it does pass is to take away from the Speakership the power . . . to appoint committees.

This means a change in system. I do not believe there are many who see how far-reaching that change may be. Consider in this connection, the mental attitude of the American citizen toward the House during the last ten years. The citizen has come to regard as normal Congressional obstruction and delay of needed legislation, and this has usually been accompanied in him by a disbelief in the adequacy of the desired law when finally enacted after long postponement. For instance, the desired changes in the railroad rate law of 1889, changes made necessary by a court decision in 1897, were reported out of committee in 1903, were enacted into law in 1905, but were made measurably effective finally in 1910. Popular disbelief in the adequacy of major laws, popular doubt of the willingness of Congress to pass effective law, has naturally bred a conviction among many that Congress is naturally not responsive to public opinion, and that, consequently, any major action by Congress must be forced not merely by means of agitation, but by prolonged and mayhap threatening agitation. Now, as the House and the Senate have lost in popular confidence, the executive branch of government has gained in it, and Presidents, conforming to the situation, veer away from the constitutional function of advising with Congress, and advance, at the opening of a new Congress, with a legislative program which an aroused and sympathetic public opinion demands shall be carried out.

A change in the system, the completion of the task of eliminating Cannonism begun at the last session of Congress, will bring the opportunity for three great developments.

First: A restoration to Congress of the normal faculty of a representative body to respond promptly to the demands of an informed and righteous public opinion.

Second: A return of power and prestige to Congress as one of the three coordinate branches of the Government.

Third: The development of a new type of Congressman, who will insist upon effective legislative action and will fully assume individual responsibility for legislation.

All three of these changes are related directly to the method of appointing committees in the House. None of the changes will have full opportunity of development if Speakers continue to appoint committees. All three changes, in some degree, will come advantageously into the life of the nation, if the House appoints its own committees.

By way of analysis, let us consider the first proposition. Why has it been necessary in the past for the public, in obtaining a needed Federal law, to work itself into a fury before Congress could be persuaded to respond? It has been necessary because, in practice, the House, and not the Senate, takes the initiative in most major legislation, demanded popularly, and the House machine, with Cannon at its head, has maintained a rigid military organization to withstand popular demand. At bottom, the secret of this organization's power was discipline, exercised in part (1) by the Speaker's arbitrary power of recognition (now in part corrected); (2) by the Speaker's presence on the Committee on Rules (now corrected); (3) by the Speaker's appointment of committees. Consider this last named power. By its use the natural, orderly growth of the House has been distorted by the Speaker. There are, for example, some fifty committees of the House, but the Speaker, who has the power of referring bills and who had, until last session, the power of preventing consideration of measures by the House, concentrated all the business of the House virtually in ten or twelve committees. This consolidation of the business into the hands of a few committees made for facility in the Speaker's control. It also diminished the number of really desirable committee places, and increased the value in which each of the places was held. It made the larger gifts in the Speaker's hands more desirable. But, most important, it enabled the Speaker to maintain perfect military discipline. And that discipline was maintained with an iron hand.

Before the day of insurgency, the chairman of an important committee was, in his relation to the Speaker, as a colonel to his general, and, in his relation to a few intimates upon his committee, as a captain to his lieutenants. The rest were privates who were encouraged, not to have opinions of their own, but to vote and act with the committee chairman, who, in turn, was known to be acting and voting as the Speaker directed. The Speaker commanded the House. If he were challenged, as he was, he punished the insurgents by leaving them off committees where they had gained rank, or reducing them in position: action taken against . . . myself and others. Before the day of insurgency the Speaker had arranged, not processes for the operation of representative government; he had formed a personal machine. After the day of insurgency another Speaker can build another personal machine, unless the House takes over the business of appointing its committees. Another Speaker, after the day of insurgency, can concentrate the business into a few committees, make the personal obligation in committee assignments paramount, and rear again a system of rewards and penalties. And just in the measure the Speaker of the future does that thing, so will necessary laws be denied, essential legislation be delayed and obstruction be practiced. For every legislative machine, once it has power, must hold that power, and to hold it the machine must use the tactics of obstruction. The machine's safety lies in negation. Standpatism is not only a belief of all legislative machines, it is also an absolutely essential element to the machine's life. The device on its emblem spells "Inaction." Therein, by the way, is the secret of Cannonism as it is found in Congress, in State legislatures and in city councils. The obstruction, delay and inadequacy in legislative action which many think are the normal, natural things for all legislative bodies are, in fact, largely practices for self-preservation by the machine. If the House will appoint its own committees, obstruction, not as a means of warfare by a minority, but obstruction as a means of control by a machine in charge of the majority, will pass. So much, then, on the opportunity of making the House responsive to popular will. . . .

It is imperative that the people see to it, by obtaining pledges from candidates for Congress, that the greater fruits of a victory over Cannonism be not lost. The House is peculiarly the political weapon of the people. It has been said often that the Senate was designed to hold back the House. It may be said also with equal warrant that the House was designed to push the Senate along. However, it was the Senate, by nature conservative, which guarded the covenant of representative government during the dark days of Cannonism. The Senate kept its procedure free. Strike the shackles from the House of Representatives, complete the work begun by the insurgents, free legislative government completely, and America will open the door upon a new era, an era which will hold not only an emancipated House, but a Senate rising, under challenge, above its inherent conservatism, and meeting, with the House, the new demands of a nation which is seeking to write into its law some measure of the nation's spirit of progress.

PROBLEM 12

# Robert M. LaFollette:
# Insurgent in Politics

Most decision makers who influenced the American political scene worked within one of the established political parties. Only with the support of the party machinery were they able to muster the votes upon which victory at the polls depended. Men who disagreed with the philosophy and the programs of the major parties often worked through third party organizations, but they seldom won executive positions in government or seats in legislatures. A few insurgent politicians like Robert M. LaFollette have managed to wrest control of an established party from its former leaders. With the party apparatus in their hands, these insurgents have won many elections particularly on the local and state levels. They have not, however, been successful in national politics.

Bob LaFollette was born in 1855 to a Wisconsin pioneer farm family; his first home was a log cabin. Admitted to the Wisconsin bar in 1880, the young lawyer defeated the Dane County party machine that same year to win an election for district attorney. He later became United States Representative, governor of Wisconsin, and United States Senator. In 1924 he was the presidential candidate of the insurgent Progressive party.

Recognizing the changing needs of the agrarian and industrial workers in the United States, LaFollette worked as both a state governor and a national legislator to make the government more responsible to the people. Throughout his long political career, "Fighting Bob" LaFollette was a progressive. He fought for measures to extend democracy, such as the direct primary, initiative, and referendum. He also sought to limit the power of large corporations and to pass child labor laws, pure food and drug acts, workmen's compensation measures, and similar legislation designed to serve the demands of a growing nation.

Problem 12 consists of two excerpts about LaFollette's career. The first, describing his difficulties as governor of Wisconsin, analyzes the feelings of various groups of citizens toward his insurgency. The second reading assesses his defeat in the 1924 presidential election. As you read, keep the following questions in mind:

**1**    What were LaFollette's goals? Why do you think he chose to fight the Republican machine in Wisconsin in order to achieve these goals? How else might LaFollette have met his objectives?

**2**    What were LaFollette's outstanding personal characteristics as a political leader? How were they suited to the role he chose to play? How did they help him to gain and maintain support?

**3**    What does LaFollette's defeat in 1924 indicate about the limits of insurgency in politics?

**4**    Was LaFollette an effective politician? Was he an effective leader? Why?

# I

## LINCOLN STEFFENS VISITS LaFOLLETTE

Lincoln Steffens was one of a group of crusading journalists whom Theodore Roosevelt tagged with the name "muckrakers." Writing about the Progressive Era in his autobiography, Steffens shows rare insight into the politics and politicians of that period. □ From *The Autobiography of Lincoln Steffens,* pp. 454–457, 459–463. Copyright, 1931, by Harcourt, Brace & World, Inc.; copyright, 1959, by Peter Steffens. Reprinted by permission of the publishers.

When, toward the end of my survey in Illinois, I sneaked up to Milwaukee to call on the men who were to display "the goods on that demagogue, Governor Bob LaFollette," I had no doubt that the man was a charlatan and a crook. And my colleagues on the magazine had none,

and the reformers and the public nationally. The reverberations of the
noise this trouble-maker had been making in his own State had been heard
all over the country, and the comment on it had painted a portrait of
LaFollette which was fixed on the public mind as it was on mine. It made
him look like two other notorious "demagogues" of the day, William
Jennings Bryan and Tom L. Johnson. My task was to get and prove the
specific charges against him and give the ready-made type a likeness to
LaFollette.

The banker, whom I called on first, was suspicious of me; he had
read something of mine. As he read over the letter I handed him and as
I talked, showing my earnest preconception, he opened up, and — LaFollette was a crooked hypocrite who stirred up the people with socialist-
anarchist ideas and hurt business. "Good," I said, "let's begin with the
evidence of his crookedness." The banker had none, but he said the
corporation attorney to whom also I had a letter could prove the dishonesty. We telephoned to him to come over. Meanwhile the banker set
out to demonstrate the other charges: hypocrisy, socialism-anarchism,
etc., and he was going fast and hot till I realized that my witness had
more feeling than facts; or if he had facts, he could not handle them.
He would start with some act of LaFollette and blow up in a rage. He
certainly hated the man, but I could not write rage. My ready-made story
of a crooked demagogue was fading when, to the banker's relief and
mine, the railroad attorney arrived with papers: evidence?

This attorney took charge at once. He said he had had full instructions from Chicago to lay the case fully before me; I was all right. When
I told him how far we had got, the banker and I, and how I wanted first
the proofs of the dishonesty alleged, he said: "Oh, no, no. You are getting
off wrong. LaFollette isn't dishonest. On the contrary, the man is dangerous precisely because he is so sincere. He's a fanatic."

"But he's a hypocrite," I appealed, fearing the loss of my great story.

"He is that," said the attorney. "He kicks about bosses and is himself a boss. He talked against the political machine and then built up an
organization that is a perfect machine."

"And an agitator?" . . .

"Yes," said the banker, "LaFollette will spread socialism all over
the world."

"But," I asked, "Milwaukee is full of socialists; are they following
LaFollette?"

"No, no," the attorney corrected. "LaFollette isn't a socialist. He
has nearly busted the socialists here, taken the votes right away from

them. The socialists are reasonable men compared with this agitator, who is more of a Populist."

"Well, then, what does he teach and what does he do?" I asked.

The attorney, with the banker sitting by frowning, impatient, presented in good order the charges against LaFollette, the measures he had furthered, the legislation passed and proposed, his political methods. Horrified himself at the items on his list and alarmed over the policy and the power of this demagogue, he delivered the indictment with emotion, force, eloquence. The only hitch was that Bob LaFollette's measures seemed fair to me, his methods democratic, his purposes right but moderate, and his fighting strength and spirit hopeful and heroic.

A day, a night, and another day of this condemnation by those men and others they introduced me to, and I was converted. Governor LaFollette's enemies convinced me that I was on the track of the best story yet, the story of a straight, able, fearless individual who was trying to achieve not merely good but representative government, and this in a State, not in a city. It was not what I came here for, but it was just what I wanted: an experience in State reform.

Returning to Chicago, I communicated with my colleagues on *McClure's*. It must have been a surprise to them, my change of attitude, but they consented. I finished up in Chicago, then called on Governor LaFollette at Madison. I saw him before he saw me, and what I saw was a powerful man who, short but solid, swift and willful in motion, in speech, in decision, gave the impression of a tall, a big, man. He had meant to be an actor; he was one always. His lines were his own, but he consciously, artfully recited them well and for effect which, like an artist, he calculated. But what I saw at my first sight of him was a sincere, ardent man who, whether standing, sitting, or in motion, had the grace of trained strength, both physical and mental. When my name was whispered to him he came at me, running. LaFollette received me eagerly as a friend, as a partisan of his, a life-saver. He had read my articles on other cities and States and assumed, of course, that I would be on his side. I did not like this. I was coming over, but it takes time to change your mind, and I was not yet over on his side.

He was not aware of my troubles, had not heard of my secret visit to Milwaukee; and he was in trouble himself. He was at a crisis in his career. Elected governor and in power, he had failed to do all that he had promised. The old machinery, by bribery, blackmail, threats, and women, had taken away from LaFollette enough of "his" legislators to defeat or amend his bills, and they were getting ready to beat him at the polls by accusing him of radicalism for proposing such measures, and of inefficiency and fraud for failing to pass them. He had no sufficient newspaper support. He feared that he could not explain it all to his own people, and he felt that the hostile opinion of the country outside his State, which the old Wisconsin machine was representing, was hurting him at home. He needed a friend; he needed just what I could give him, national, non-partisan support. . . . His part was to lay it all out before me, himself, his acts, the circumstances, his reasons, excuses, purposes, and he did that conscientiously, in order and with ability, giving as well as his enemies did afterward their interpretations and their charges and their joy in his faults and failures.

As he went on with his story, I took notes — enough for a book — the open book of an ambitious young man who, fitted in the schools and University of Wisconsin with the common, patriotic conception of his country and his government, discovered bit by bit what the facts were, and, shocked, set out to fight for democracy, justice, honesty. He set out ambitiously on a public career, encountered a local boss in a Federal office, and appealed over his head to the people of his home county to be nominated and elected district attorney. This was his first offense; he was irregular; he defied the machine of his (Republican) party. The politicians said that Bob LaFollette worked on the delegates and the voters at night, under cover of darkness. True. And when he felt the power and suffered the methods and the lying attacks of the party and its backing higher up, he continued to work under cover and constantly, like the politicians; but also he worked in the open, day and night. His method, in brief, was to go around to towns and cross-roads, make long, carefully stated speeches of fact, and appealing to the idealism of patriotism, watch the audience for faces, mostly young faces which he thought showed inspiration. These he invited to come to him afterward; he showed them what the job was, asked them if they would do their part in their district; and so he built up an organized following so responsive to him that it was called a machine. As it was — a powerful political machine which came to control the Republican Party in Wisconsin. The Stalwarts, as the old machine men and their business backers were called, became irregulars; they voted against and fought their party. They united with the old machine Democrats to beat their party. But LaFollette drew into it democratic Democrats and independents enough to make a majority for the Republicans, who came thus in Wisconsin to represent the people.

That was Bob LaFollette's crime. When Governor LaFollette returned to his State one way and I by another route, I called on the Stalwarts for facts, provable charges, and on LaFollette only for his specific answers or admissions. As in Milwaukee, so in Madison, the indictments withered. They fell back to his one real sin: that he had taken the Republican party away from the corrupters of it and led it to stand for — what? I said above that it represented the people, but it did that only in the sense that it labored for and gradually achieved the very moderate aims of LaFollette, a liberal, and the liberals. When I pointed this out to such men as Old Boss Keyes [Wisconsin Stalwart Republican boss] and Philip Spooner [a Keyes lieutenant] they were stumped. They bade me go to Milwaukee again and see the men there who knew things, especially a certain attorney who had written a book against . . . [LaFollette].

Since they did not know that I had been to Milwaukee and I could not go away to write without having it known that I had seen Milwaukee, I went there as openly as I could. Stalwarts called on me, offered me — rage, indignation, allegations I had investigated. As I received their stuff credulously at first, then began to ask questions, they spread the report that I was "no fool" and, apparently, "put up a job on me." Anyway, against my wish, several of them invited, urged, me to go with them to see that certain attorney who knew so much. I refused. One day I was invited to luncheon in the Hotel Pfister. My hosts, smiling at and nudging one another, led me through the barroom and stopped suddenly to present me to the attorney whom they regarded as so clever and well up on the facts. There was a crowd in the barroom, and the crowd closed in on us to see the fun.

"Why haven't you come to see me?" the attorney asked, smiling around the circle of listeners.

"Oh," I answered, "I have read your book. I see that you know, but I feel that I should know something for certain before I trouble a witness like you."

"Don't be afraid of me," he laughed. "Ask me anything you like. I'll answer you, now."

I was up against it. The crowd snickered, and I saw that I had to meet the challenge and ask a question. The underworld have to think you are "wise," or your writings won't "go." I thought a moment, eyeing my man, and I remembered that there was one alleged scandal which I had learned all about and which everybody there knew all about. I asked my opponent to tell me the truth of that matter. He began, as I had expected, to tell me the scandalous story as it first appeared, before the investigation, and I encouraged him by my exclamations to give it me all wrong, as he did.

"Oh, so that's the way of it!" I said. "I didn't know that! Nobody ever told me that!" And all the time the crowd was laughing, winking, and driving him to "fill me up" more and more. I waited till he was all through; then I said: "I am amazed at your story. It's so much worse than I had any idea. If that's so, LaFollette is a damned rascal. But listen now, this is the way I have got it after a rather careful investigation." And I told it as it was and as that crowd and that witness knew it was, with references to the records and proofs.

Before I had finished, the audience was still and cold, they were looking at the attorney as if he were caught stealing, and he, angry, turned on me and demanded: "If you know all about it, why the hell do you ask me?"

"Because," I answered, "I have heard that you have the evidence on LaFollette, that I must see and listen to and believe you; so, when you stalled me for the amusement of this crowd, I decided to take the chance to test the reliability of the witness."

The laugh was on him, and there was a laugh. It swept him out of his anger.

"Come on and have a drink," he called and so saved his face—a little. I never saw him again. . . .

Bob LaFollette was restoring representative government in Wisconsin, and by his oratory and his fierce dictatorship and his relentless conspicuous persistence he was making his people understand—all of them, apparently, not only the common people whom he preferred, but the best people too; they also knew. They might denounce him, they might lie to the stranger, but in their heart of hearts they knew. It was a great experiment, LaFollette's: State reform that began in the capital of the State and spread out close to the soil. It was opposed by the cities, just as city reform was opposed by the States, but the startling thing—even though I expected it—was how this State reform encountered also the resistance of the Federal government. And just as . . . [city] reformers had been forced to carry their fight up out of the cities into the States whence the trail of the serpent led, so Governor LaFollette, having carried his State several times, found that he had to go on up to the Senate.

The trail of corruption is the road to success for the reformer as well as for other men. He won the next election for governor and then ran for and was elected to the U.S. Senate. He did not rush off to the Senate right away. It was characteristic of him that he remained as governor months after he was promoted to the Senate. He stuck to his post till he finished and forced the Legislature to pass all his pending measures.

Then and not till then did he go on, where I saw I had to go, to the head of the system of the American government in — Washington. His career there, as in his own State, is the story of the heroism it takes to fight in America for American ideals.

# II

## LaFOLLETTE AND THE CAMPAIGN OF 1924

Robert M. LaFollette, in the presidential election of 1924, received more popular votes than any other third party candidate had received until that time. Although the Progressive party fell far short of victory, its programs attracted millions of farmers, workers, and other Americans who were disgruntled with major party leadership.  □  "What LaFollette Won." New York: *The Nation*, Volume 120, Number 3105, January 7, 1925, p. 5.

Senator LaFollette has let it be known that the third-party organization will carry on . . . . Well he may, with the complete returns of the November election at last before him.

We are obsessed in this country by electoral-college figures. "LaFollette could carry only his own home State," people say, and shake their heads. As if that meant anything! In fact, he polled close to five million votes — 4,822,319 outside of Louisiana, where his adherents were counted among the "scattering." That is more than either Roosevelt or Taft polled in 1912, and it is surely far too many to justify the hasty newspaper predictions of death for the movement.

It is worth while to pause long enough, even two months after election, to discover just what the LaFollette vote amounted to. It is a little misleading to say that it was greater than Roosevelt's or Taft's vote, for we have woman suffrage now, and the total vote is substantially larger. LaFollette did not win a larger proportion of the popular vote than Roosevelt and Taft won in 1912. He had 17 per cent of the votes, Davis 29, and Coolidge 54 per cent. Eight years ago Roosevelt had 27 per cent, and Taft 24. But Debs, in 1912, polled only 6 per cent, and he more than Roosevelt represented the attempt to form a new producers' party based upon the common interests of the city workers and the farmers.

The third-party idea has gained in strength in this last decade, and has struck roots into the soil. Whereas Roosevelt attempted to win the Republican Party away from its old leaders and make it into a personal following, LaFollette sought to express a mass movement. Roosevelt had with him almost as many of the regular party bosses as were lined up against him. LaFollette bucked the machine all along the line. Only in Wisconsin, his own State and the single State he carried, did he have the advantage of control of a party organization and machinery.

Analyzed by sections of the country the LaFollette-Wheeler Progressive vote is even more significant and impressive. Count out the solid South, the border States, and the conservative Northeast, and Senator LaFollette ran well ahead of Davis. The most striking feature of any such analysis is, of course, the overwhelming, nation-wide character of the Coolidge sweep. The little Yankee in the White House somehow caught the imagination of the country; he expressed its essential conservatism and soothed its fears, and while his vote of 15,718,789 was somewhat less than Harding's crashing total he received the largest plurality ever recorded for a Presidential candidate in America. In New England and the Northeast [New York, Pennsylvania, New Jersey, Delaware] he actually won a larger proportion of the votes than Davis did in the South [including, with the solid South, Maryland, West Virginia, Kentucky, Tennessee, Oklahoma, and Missouri]. West of the Mississippi he received nearly two votes to every one for LaFollette, and more than three to every one for John W. Davis.

. . . [In] the great region west of the Mississippi, which includes twenty-two of the forty-eight States of the Union, the third party is now the second party, and the Democratic Party, already disintegrating after the blow of 1920, is fighting for mere existence. As important is the showing in the East [where LaFollette won 13 per cent of the total to Coolidge's 61 per cent]. Not for a half century has a new party made such inroads into that center of conservatism. Some writers like to compare the Populist movement, a flash in the pan, with the agrarian movement which was a part of LaFollette's support; but at its peak in 1892 the Populist Party polled only 16,000 votes in New York State, where this year LaFollette rallied 475,000—more than came out for him in Wisconsin itself. Considering the utter lack of organization at the start and the deliberate treachery of the labor unions in New York City, which turned to Davis at the critical moment, that is a remarkably encouraging showing. The labor leaders of the metropolis may be mere appanages of Tammany; the American Federation of Labor may be in the hands of visionless conservatives; the farmers may lack organization; but the vote of the 1924 election proves that there is a rank-and-file progressive movement in the country. It is not on the threshold of victory yet; there is hard work ahead; but the foundation is laid.

PROBLEM 13

# Huey P. Long:
# Agitator as Politician

The time and circumstance of Huey Long's political career made Long different as a political agitator from either Samuel Adams or Eugene Debs. Adams, a Harvard graduate who appealed to the élite of colonial society as well as to the masses, helped trigger the American Revolution. Debs, labor leader and socialist, worked selflessly to lead his followers toward his own vision of a better society. Long, champion of the discontented people of Louisiana, determinedly climbed the political ladder to become the most powerful leader in the state during the late 1920's and early 1930's.

When Huey Long came into prominence in Louisiana, the legislatures and governors were supported by money from big business and did next to nothing to meet the pressing social problems of the state. Long's program, influenced by a backwoods type of populism, reflected distrust of the wealthy planters and "big city" politicians who controlled the state. Entering state politics in 1918 when he was elected to the post of Public Service Commissioner, Long quickly attracted wide attention and acclaim by attacking the Standard Oil Company for its connection with the New Orleans political ring. He failed to capture the governorship in 1924 but won the post four years later. From that time until his death in 1935, Long was one of the most controversial figures in American political history.

Huey Long was successful at the outset of his political career because he was forceful and imaginative at a time when the state government was complacent. He kept his promises to provide new roads, bridges, and educational opportunities—all badly needed in Louisiana. Grateful voters elected Long to the United States Senate in 1930, but he did not go to Washington until two years later. He retained the governorship of Louisiana until he could place a hand-picked successor in the governor's chair. Only then did he take up his work in the Senate.

By 1933 the depression had left one out of four workers in the United States without a job. President Franklin Roosevelt's New Deal legislation sought to meet the emergency, but widespread suffering continued. It was in this context that Huey Long attempted to capture the attention of the entire country. He appealed for a redistribution of the wealth and organized Share-Our-Wealth clubs throughout the nation. These clubs, claiming up to five million members, supported a number of Long's legislative proposals by which he hoped to relieve the suffering caused by the depression.

Although Long supported Franklin Roosevelt's successful bid for the presidency in 1932, he soon broke with the administration when it failed to agree with his ideas for the redistribution of wealth. His denunciation of Roosevelt came with increasing boldness. Despite growing opposition to his program and power in Louisiana, Long announced his candidacy for the presidency in August 1935. While political experts considered his chances of victory slight, they agreed that he could be a threat to Roosevelt's re-election. Huey Long never posed that threat; he was assassinated in the state capitol at Baton Rouge on September 8, 1935. His assassin, Dr. Carl Weiss, was quickly gunned down by the host of bodyguards who constantly surrounded Long.

As you read, keep the following questions in mind:

**1**   What was the setting in which Long operated? How did the setting contribute to his success?

**2**   What tactics did Long use? What appeals did he make? What sorts of people responded to these appeals?

**3**   Do you think that Long and LaFollette failed to gain national recognition for similar reasons?

**4**   Could Long's leadership techniques succeed on the national scene?

# I

## IN PRAISE OF HUEY LONG

The Share-Our-Wealth movement, inspired by Huey Long, sought legislation which would guarantee a minimum annual income of $5000 to every family in the United States. One of Long's most steadfast supporters in this movement was the Reverend Gerald L. K. Smith. Smith worked with Long in the Share-Our-Wealth movement and succeeded to the leadership of the clubs after Long's assassination. The excerpt that follows is an editorial by Smith in praise of Long's program. □ Gerald L. K. Smith, "How Come Huey Long?" New York: *The New Republic,* Volume 82, Number 1054, February 13, 1935, pp. 14–15.

Nine years ago [1926], Louisiana was a feudal state. Until that time it was ruled by the feudal lords in New Orleans and on the big plantations: the cotton kings, lumber kings, rice kings, oil kings, sugar kings, molasses kings, banana kings, etc. The state was just a "mainland" of the territory. The common people in New Orleans were ruled, domineered over and bulldozed by a political organization known as the Old Regulars. The great mass of people in the city and the country worked like slaves or else lived in an isolation that excluded opportunity. Labor unions were very weak and the assembly of workers was prohibited in most industrial centers. It was not uncommon for labor organizers to be beaten or assassinated.

The great corporations ruled the state and pushed the tax burden onto the poor. The Chambers of Commerce spent money in the North urging industry to come South for cheap labor. Illiteracy was as common as peonage. The commissary plan was in force in mills and on plantations; it kept the workers from receiving cash and left them always in debt to the employer. The highway system was a series of muddy lanes with antique ferries and narrow bridges with high toll charges. Great forests sold for a dollar an acre, to be "slaughtered" and removed with nothing left to enrich the lives of stranded . . . population [of the area]. Families north of New Orleans were forced to pay an $8 toll to cross Lake Pontchartrain into New Orleans and return.

Of course, we had our grand and glorious aristocracy, plantation mansions, the annual Mardi Gras festival, horse races, and those staunch defenders of the old South, the newspapers. Of course, the old Louisiana aristocracy, with its lords, dukes and duchesses, had to be preserved, regardless of what happened to the people. State institutions constituted a disgrace. The insane were strapped, put into stocks and beaten. The penitentiary was an abyss of misery, hunger and graft. The State University had 1,500 students with a "C" rating. Most of the young people were too poor to attend Tulane, the only big university in the state. Ten thousand aristocrats ruled the state while 2,000,000 common people wallowed in slavery with no representation in the affairs of the state. Half of the children could not read or write. Little consideration was given to Negro education. Professional training was available only to the sons of the privileged.

Huey Long grew up in the pine woods of Winn Parish. He had witnessed the sale of trees worth $10 each for $1 an acre. He was sensitive to injustice. He knew the difficulty of receiving a higher education. He seemed to have an intuitive appreciation of ideal social conditions. At the age of twenty, his Share the Wealth ideal was fixed in his mind. Shortly after, he announced his ambition to become Governor. He was ridiculed, patronized and pitied. True enough, he was a mustang—rough, wild, vigorous, and at the same time mysteriously intelligent. At thirty, he was the best lawyer in Louisiana. He had the surface manners of a demagogue, but the depth of a statesman. This dual nature accounts for many of his victories. He wins like a demagogue and delivers like a statesman. His capacity for work was unlimited. He waded through mud, drove along dusty highways, and soon became the poor man's best friend. After fifteen hours of hard work, he could recover completely with three hours of sleep. He recognized the value of entertainment in leading these sad, enslaved people out of bondage. He is Louisiana's greatest humorist. It was his wedge, but behind that wedge was a deep sympathy and a tender understanding of the needs of his people.

In 1928 he was elected Governor. He had promised many things that even his staunchest admirers questioned his ability to deliver. He moved to Baton Rouge, tore down the old Governor's mansion, built a new one, built a new capitol, built new university buildings, refused to entertain socially, attended no banquets, snubbed the elite and opened the mansion to the muddy feet of his comrades. He offended the sensibilities of the tender sons and daughters of privilege. He whipped bankers into line, he struck blow after blow at peonage, he gave orders to the Standard Oil Company, the bank trust and the feudal lords. Society matrons, lottery kings, gamblers, exclusive clubs and—not to be forgotten—leading clergymen with sensitive flocks joined hands to impeach this "wild," "horrible," "terrible," "bad" man. The war was on. Impeachment proceedings failed. State senators, representatives, and appointees began to obey like humble servants — not in fear, but quite as anxious parents obey a great physician who prescribes for a sick child. He was recognized by friend and foe as the smartest man in Louisiana.

Severance taxes were levied on oil, gas, lumber, and other natural resources, which made possible free schoolbooks for all children, black and white, rich and poor, in public and private schools. Telephone rates were cut, gas rates were cut, electric rates were cut; night schools were opened up and 149,000 adults were taught to read and write. Then came free ferries, new free bridges, 5,000 miles of paved and improved roads (six years ago [1929], we had only seventeen miles of pavement in Louisiana); a free medical school was built, as fine as any in the country. Free school buses were introduced, the assembly of workers for organization was guaranteed, new advantages were created for the deaf, the blind, the widows, the orphans and the insane, the penitentiary was modernized, traveling libraries were introduced and improved highways were forced through impassable swamps. Recently poll taxes were abolished, giving franchise to 300,000 who had never voted. Legislation has been passed, removing all small homes and farms from the tax roll. This means that 95 percent of the Negro population will pay no taxes and 70 percent of the total population will be tax free. This transfers the tax burden from the worker to those who profit by his labor. . . .

In the midst of all this, Huey Long was elected to the United States Senate, and began to preach in Washington what he had been practising in Louisiana. He made the first real speech and introduced the first real bill for the actual redistribution of wealth.

On February 3, 1934, he founded the Share Our Wealth Society and called on the American people to organize in order to accomplish the following objectives:

1. Limitation of poverty to a minimum of a $5,000 family estate.
2. Limitation of wealth to a maximum of $10,000,000.
3. Free higher education for all, with a mental test instead of the tuition test. If men in the army can be fed, boarded and clothed while we teach them how to kill, we can do as much for the best minds while they are being trained to live.
4. Employment for all by the shortening of hours.
5. Full compensation for veterans.
6. Old-age pensions
7. Great national . . . programs to absorb the unemployed. . . .

Our newspapers have given out the report that Senator Long is our dictator. The fact of the case is that the power to govern in Louisiana has been transferred from the feudal lords and their servile newspapers to the common people who elected a man to lead them and are standing by him. At the close of the Legislature this summer, long stories were written about Huey Long's puppet Governor and Legislature. The facts are these: At the close of the Legislature, the program was submitted to the people for a referendum and by a vote of 7 to 1 every major thing accomplished by the Legislature was approved.

Demagogues do not decide to educate their people. They thrive on ignorance. They may promise the same things that Huey Long promises, but they never deliver them. He keeps all of his campaign promises. We, who follow him, adore him and consider ourselves flattered when he asks our help. He never lies to us. He never uses the fall-guy method of protecting himself. He takes the blame for our mistakes. . . .

Huey Long is the greatest headline writer I have ever seen. His circulars attract, bite, sting and convince. It is difficult to imagine what would happen in America if every human being were to read one Huey Long circular on the same day. As a mass-meeting speaker, his equal has never been known in America. His knowledge of national and international affairs, as well as local affairs, is uncanny. He seems to be equally at home with all subjects, such as shipping, railroads, banking, Biblical literature, psychology, merchandising, utilities, sports, Oriental affairs, international treaties, South American affairs, world history, the Constitution of the United States, the Napoleonic Code, construction, higher education, flood control, cotton, lumber, sugar, rice, alphabetical relief agencies. Besides this, I am convinced that he is the greatest political strategist alive. Huey Long is a superman. . . . He abstains from alcohol, he uses no tobacco; he is strong, youthful and enthusiastic. Hostile communities and individuals move toward him like an avalanche once they see him and hear him speak. His greatest recommendation is that we who know him best, love him most.

# II

## A SOUTHERN JOURNALIST'S OPPOSING VIEWS

Hodding Carter, editor of the *Delta Democrat Times* in Greenville, Mississippi, watched the rise of Huey Long in neighboring Louisiana and wrote the following view of Long's tactics and regime. □ Hodding Carter, "How Come Huey Long?" New York: *The New Republic,* Volume 82, Number 1054, February 13, 1935, pp. 11-13.

Under the spreading loblolly pine tree, the village skeptic stands pretty much alone, and very quiet in his skepticism. Apart from him, his fellow villagers and their country kinsmen loll and listen. The Louisiana sun beats down impartially upon them and upon the red-faced, stentorian-voiced exhorter, whose blue shirt is soaked with perspiration. His flailing, prophetically extended arms are raised in benediction, with a swift detour to wipe the sweat from his face. His voice, amplified through the loudspeaker on the sound truck, trembles with histrionic emotion.

"All of you that ain't got *four* suits of clothes, raise your hands," he bellows.

Five hundred pairs of arms shoot skyward.

"I thought so—I thought so, brethren. Now all of you that ain't got *three* suits of clothes, raise your hands."

Again a thousand arms reach to the sky.

"Just like I knew, brethren. Oh, blessed are the poor, but what a row they have to hoe. Now all of you that ain't got *two* suits of clothes, raise your hands."

For the third time, the arms reach convulsively, almost triumphantly into the air.

"Not even *two* suits of clothes. Oh, my brethren, J. P. Morgan has two suits of clothes. He has a hundred times two suits of clothes. And that ain't all. Now all of you all that ain't got even *one* suit of clothes— one single suit of clothes that the pants match the coat—raise your hands."

Once more the thousand hands are raised, and a shout almost like a thanksgiving comes from the mass of suitless listeners who are living in the word-paradise and under the paralyzing dictatorship of Huey P. Long.

The coat-and-pants speaker is Gerald L. K. Smith—the Reverend Gerald L. K. Smith—high priest and prophet of Senator Long's Share Our Wealth movement. When he concludes his two-hour speech against Wall Street and the assorted opponents of Huey Long, there will be five hundred new members of the society. Five hundred gaunt, grinning farmers and small-town ne'er-do-wells will file beside the sound truck and sign the cards that automatically make them members of the National Share Our Wealth Society of Huey Long.

Huey has more than Wall Street on the run in Louisiana, and the legislative travesties by which he has accomplished his complete dictatorship are costing a pretty penny, though not at the direct expense of his fellow wealth-sharers; for theirs is not the eventual day of reckoning in a state where business is terrorized and where the public debt of nearly $150,000,000 is the third greatest in the union. Huey Long is now the sole dispenser of boons and headaches in the Louisiana duchy. For a righteous Share Our Wealth member, things are rosy. Huey has reduced the automobile licenses, especially for farmers. He has ordained a two-thousand-dollar homestead exemption, provided, of course, that other taxes bring in revenue to keep the machine wheels greased. He has granted a two-year debt moratorium—federal obligations excluded—and as judges of whether individual moratoria should be granted he has appointed loyal legislators in direct opposition to the state Constitution. The one-dollar poll tax is a thing of the past. Add all that to paved roads, free schoolbooks and a continual taxation harrying of the Standard Oil and the public utilities, with imminent though yet unrealized rate reductions, and you get a pretty good idea of why the doctrine of wealth sharing has taken hold among the poor whites, who constitute the majority of Louisiana's electorate.

Through such benefactions, Huey claims to have "Mr. Roosevelt's depression" on the run in Louisiana. He has managed to obtain such powers as were never before won by any politician in the United States. For, at the present time, Huey Long has sole control of fixing assessments in the state. He can decide through his own state bar association, created by the legislature, who shall and who shall not be a practising member of the Louisiana bar. Through an ironically named Civil Service Commission, he can remove, and already has removed, elected or appointed officials of political subdivisions of the state, both municipal and parish. The State Supreme Court, his by a consistent four-to-three margin, can legalize anything he has enacted, and his secret state police force, its identity and numbers known only to the administration, can take you out of your home whenever it likes and hold you incommunicado on whatever charge may be necessary. . . .

The organization of a Share Our Wealth club is as pleasingly effortless as its promised benefits. A prospective member has only to obtain, free of charge, a membership card, following one of the Reverend Gerald's rousing meetings. There are no dues-strings attached, no matter what the newspapers say. Blazoned across the card is the caption "Share Our Wealth Society—Every Man a King." One merely has to fill in one's name, or have one's friend oblige in case the ability to write is lacking as it often is, and one's address, age and the names and addresses of other prospective members. And just think—this card will be filed in Senator Huey Long's offices in Washington, D.C! We'll be on the inside track when the great day arrives. Moreover, each member has the opportunity of being president or secretary of a Share Our Wealth club. There are no treasurers, as yet. These high offices can be attained through persuading two or three others in one's neighborhood to fill out cards and send them to Washington. By getting these members, a man can become president of the club thus formed, for as Brother Smith opines, a Share Our Wealth club has much of the Biblical in it: "Wherever two or three are gathered together in My name, there am I in the midst of them." Besides, says Huey, the Gideons had but two men when they organized, and "Three Tailors of Tooley Street drew the Magna Carta of England."

On Sundays and holidays the members can hold Share Our Wealth parades, with American flags and slightly contradictory banners bearing the slogan "Every Man a King." The presidents of the neighborhood locals can vie with each other in making speeches that are earnest if imperfect replicas of Reverend Smith's evangelistic pronouncements or Huey's signed messages in his roaring weekly, The American Progress. In between times, they can improve the shining hour by reading, learning and inwardly digesting the countless Progress stories describing the horrors of the concentration of wealth. Also, when one of the many Louisiana elections for everything from coroner to Governor comes up, they can satisfy themselves by questioning the candidates as to their opinions of the Share Our Wealth program. The independent or anti-Long candidate in the country precincts thus can be placed in a distressing dilemma. If he is so foolhardy as to answer "poppycock" he can kiss a large and solid block of votes goodbye. If he endorses the plan, grudgingly or even enthusiastically, he is still viewed with skepticism, for an alert wealth-sharer will point out that since he is fighting Huey, his wealth-sharing support is only a vote-getting scheme—why he's a demagogue, that's what he is.

Undoubtedly, the Share Our Wealth program is the most brilliantly conceived of all of Huey Long's many political brain children. Its appeal is unanswerable on the stump. Its clever employment of truth and half-truth as a foundation for its promises of plenty for the poor and its criticism of unrestricted wealth for the wealthy make the odds pretty high against the supporters of things-as-they-are, or even the sincere but less munificent economic trail blazers. No one questions Brother Smith's declaration that millions are unemployed, near starvation and dependent on New Deal doles. There is no rebuttal to his statement that America is a land of plenty, with enough supplies to feed, goods to clothe and building materials to house in comfort every man, woman and child.

Though his figures may be a few billions out of the way, no one denies that a tremendous amount of the nation's wealth is in the hands of a few, while the many "ain't got even one suit of clothes."

Of course, there is nothing new in the human fundamentals to which Huey and the Reverend appeal, or in the economic reforms they advocate. Class consciousness, envy of wealth and a desire for the creature comforts of life are strong in the United States today, as they have been strong in every nation in every age. This is especially true of the poor whites of the South, those near-disenfranchised, lethargic and doomed relics of a ruinous agricultural system. Old-age pensions, unemployment insurance, a balance of supply and demand, wealth spread—these have been the war cries of modern economists long before the New Deal was supposed to begin its attack on Big Business. But where the student of economics presents his suggestions through an impersonal, systematic theory, whose appeal is primarily to the rational, Huey and his high priest strike home to the emotions, the hates and the desires, the superstitions of the underprivileged poor-white class.

Reverend Smith, who, next to Huey Long and Mississippi's [Senator Theodore Gilmore] Bilbo, is probably the most talented rabble rouser in the South, can in an instant switch his mighty voice from piteously picturing Christ on the Cross to calling the local anti-Long leaders a "bunch of dirty, thieving drunkards." Escorted by force from one parish by a determined group of anti-administrationists, with the heeded warning not to turn up again, he bobs up in the next parish with a vitriolic attack on his "persecutors" and proceeds upon his Christian way, describing the wife of a former Governor, who fought Long until her recent death, as "two jumps ahead of the insane asylum," and calling upon any hostile member in the crowd to "shoot me while I stand here helpless," his arms outstretched as though pinned to a cross and his sound truck surrounded by vigilant state police in plainclothes and uniform.

Reverend Smith has not confined his political and economic proselyting to Louisiana alone. He has gone into Mississippi, Alabama, Arkansas, preaching Share Our Wealth and organizing societies. Weekly The American Progress reports thousands of new members. Huey and the Reverend Smith claim that there are now five million members in the United States. Divide this assertion by five or ten, and you still have a sizable—and in Louisiana a distinctly militant—group of zealots. The American Progress keeps hammering away at concentrated wealth, the chain stores, the national administration and the assorted opposition to Huey's rule in Louisiana. Under senatorial . . . [franking privilege],

Huey floods the nation with similar masterpieces, whose literary and ethical level is but slightly higher than those that The Progress presents for fifty cents a year—and don't bother about paying, we deduct printing expenses from the payrolls. Every person in the United States who can read, and many who can't, know at least vaguely who Huey Long is and what he is driving at.

"Wall Street and its newspapers, and the radio liars say this is a scheme to make money for your friend, Huey Long," shouts Reverend Smith. "They'd kill him if they could, my brethren. And they're going to have to kill him to keep him from helping you. As God is my judge, the only way they will keep Huey Long from the White House is to kill him. But when they do, his great work will go marching on. Share, brothers, share, and don't let those white-livered skunks laugh at you."

PROBLEM 14

# Arthur H. Vandenberg:
# Senate Leader

Regarded as one of the leaders of the isolationist bloc in the Senate through the 1930's, Republican Senator Arthur H. Vandenberg of Michigan underwent a most dramatic and significant conversion to internationalism in 1941. He expressed his feelings in his diary: "My convictions regarding international cooperation and collective security for peace took firm form on the afternoon of the Pearl Harbor attack. That day ended isolationism for any realist." Senator Vandenberg's career illustrates how a legislator can profoundly affect national policies.

Arthur Vandenberg was born in 1884 of a poor family. Forced to leave the University of Michigan for financial reasons, he became a cub reporter for the Grand Rapids *Herald* and rose to the position of editor and publisher before becoming a United States Senator. Vandenberg held no other public office. He was first appointed to the Senate in 1928 to fill an unexpired term and was subsequently re-elected every six years until his death in 1951.

Senator Vandenberg's leadership was most conspicuous in the area of foreign affairs. Even after war broke out in Europe in 1939, Vandenberg consistently voted against any measure that he felt would lead the country into the conflict. Once the United States was attacked, however, Vandenberg threw his full weight behind the development of a truly bipartisan foreign policy.

After the war it was Vandenberg, more than any other Republican in the Senate, who embraced the Truman administration's foreign aid program. He particularly supported the European Recovery Plan (Marshall Plan) and the Economic Cooperation Administration, by which the United States hoped to stimulate economic recovery in western Europe with technical assistance and capital investment. In debating this program he crossed swords with his close friend and Senate colleague, Robert Taft of Ohio. In answer to Taft's opposition, Vandenberg said: "I should think that the Senator from Ohio would join me among the very first. . . . If he found that those [people] with whom we were co-operating were doing what we had contemplated and hoped for . . . he would be the first to say it was a golden opportunity to continue this program." Taft's resolution to reduce the appropriation for the Marshall Plan was defeated 56 to 31.

Vandenberg was thoroughly accepted in the Republican party, and he was a member of the inner group of established Senators who set the rules of the Senate. With this influence, he led his party and his nation along new paths. He devoted much of his energy to the task of persuading his colleagues to follow the leadership of the Democratic President. At the same time, he helped the American public realize its new tasks in the postwar world.

The readings in Problem 14 deal with several aspects of Vandenberg's career. The first illustrates his isolationist sentiments in the midst of the world crisis in 1939. The second, indicating the extent to which his attitudes changed, comes from a speech supporting the Marshall Plan, which he delivered in 1948. The final reading assesses Vandenberg's role as a leader. As you read, think about the following questions:

**1** Why do you think Vandenberg changed his position on foreign affairs during the period from 1939 to 1945?

**2** How did Vandenberg's position in the inner circle of the Senate help him as a leader? Do you see any traces of the agitator, theorist, or political manipulator in him?

**3** What were Vandenberg's outstanding political skills? Were they particularly useful inside or outside the formal structure of decision making?

**4** How did Vandenberg's role as a leader differ from that of LaFollette?

# I

## VANDENBERG AS AN ISOLATIONIST

Senator Vandenberg addressed the Senate on February 27, 1939. ☐ Arthur H. Vandenberg, "Peace or War for America." New York: *Vital Speeches of the Day*, Volume 5, Number 12, April 1, 1939, pp. 354–355.

One of the dangerous misconceptions which are taking possession of our thinking in some quarters is the notion that we can thrust ourselves into foreign quarrels and mold alien destiny by methods "short of war." That is the treacherous phrase — "short of war." We hear it in high places. We can assert ourselves in respect to the clashes and the conflicts and the conquests of other peoples, . . . but we shall always stop "short of war."

That, Mr. President, is a deeply dangerous infatuation. Perhaps there are some things, Heaven willing, which we can do "short of war" in attempting to influence the course of events in foreign controversies which find other nations preparing to fight for their own objectives: but it is an utterly treacherous reliance. When we once assert ourselves as partisan in one of these foreign collisions of self-interest we have taken a step which may put subsequent destiny entirely beyond our own control. If we take the next step in the form of some one-sided punitive action or support we definitely are no longer in control of destiny. We may still complacently and short-sightedly tell ourselves that we intend to stop "short of war," but we are unfortunately no longer in control of these tragic traffic lights. If the answering reprisals become intolerable, we have no alternative but to resist them by force of arms. Regardless of our original intention to stop "short of war," we may too easily find ourselves plunged into war itself.

We should never take the first step, Mr. President, unless we are deliberately and consciously ready and willing to take the final step if it becomes inevitable. Otherwise we invite not only humiliation but also the complete disintegration of our international influence.

There is no such thing as a partial interference in the quarrels of other nations which can dependably stop "short of war." I am speaking not only of the application of economic sanctions, I am speaking equally of provocative speech which ignores the time-tested admonitions in Washington's Farewell Address; and I want to read . . . from that address:

"The nation which indulges towards another an habitual hatred, or an habitual fondness, is in some degree a slave. It is a slave to its animosity or to its affection, either of which is sufficient to lead it astray from its duty and its interest. Antipathy in one nation against another disposes each more readily to offer insult and injury, to lay hold of slight causes of umbrage, and to be haughty and intractable when accidental or trifling occasions of dispute occur. Hence, frequent collisions, obstinate, envenomed, and bloody contests. The nation prompted by ill will and resentment sometimes impels to war the government contrary to the best calculations of policy."

Still quoting from the Farewell Address:

"The government sometimes participates in the national propensity and adopts through passion what reason would reject; at other times it makes the animosity of the nation subservient to projects of hostility, instigated by pride, ambition, and other sinister and pernicious motives."

Listen:

"The peace often, sometimes perhaps the liberty, of nations has been the victim."

Ah, Mr. President, this address may be 150 years old but, like the law of gravity, it is as constant in its wisdom and accuracy today as it was the day it was uttered.

# II

## A MIND CHANGED

After the United States entered World War II, Senator Vandenberg worked tirelessly in behalf of a lasting world peace. Speaking on March 1, 1948, Vandenberg reflected the change which occurred in his approach to foreign policy by supporting the Economic Cooperation Administration. □ Arthur H. Vandenberg, "The Economic Cooperation Administration." New York: *Vital Speeches of the Day*, Volume 14, Number 11, March 15, 1948, pp. 322-323, 329.

Mr. President, with the unanimous approval of the Senate Foreign Relations Committee, I report the Economic Cooperation act of 1948 in its perfected text. In the name of peace, stability, and freedom it deserves prompt passage. In the name of intelligent American self-interest it envisions a mighty undertaking worthy of our faith. It is an economic act — but economics usually control national survivals these days. The act itself asserts that "disruption following in the wake of war is not contained by national frontiers." It asserts that "the existing situation in Europe endangers the establishment of a lasting peace, the general welfare and national interest of the United States, and the attainment of the objectives of the United Nations."

Every Senator knows that these dangers are even greater than they were when those words were written only two short weeks ago. The fate of Czechoslovakia, where any semblance of democracy has just been gutted by subversive conquest, underscores this solemn thesis. The kindred fate of brave little Finland may be adding to the ominous score this very afternoon even while we debate an axiom, namely, that aggressive communism threatens all freedom and all security, whether in the Old World or in the New, when it puts free peoples anywhere in chains.

The act asserts sound doctrine when it says that it is "the policy of the people of the United States to sustain and strengthen principles of individual liberty, free institutions and genuine independence through assistance to those countries of Europe which participate in a joint recovery program based upon self-help and mutual cooperation." Mr. President, this act may well become a welcome beacon in the world's dark night, but if a beacon is to be lighted at all it had better be lighted before it is too late.

Nevertheless, Mr. President, the decision which here concerns the Senate is the kind that tries men's souls. I understand and share the anxieties involved. It would be a far happier circumstance if we could close our eyes to reality, comfortably retire within our bastions, and dream of an isolated and prosperous peace. But that which was once our luxury would now become our folly. This is too plain to be persuasively denied in a foreshortened, atomic world. We must take things as they are.

The greatest nation on earth either justifies or surrenders its leadership. We must choose. There are no blueprints to guarantee results. We are entirely surrounded by calculated risks. I profoundly believe that the pending program is the best of these risks. I have no quarrel with those who disagree, because we are dealing with imponderables. But I am bound to say to those who disagree that they have not escaped to safety by rejecting or subverting this plan. They have simply fled to other risks, and I fear far greater ones. For myself, I can only say that I prefer my choice of responsibilities.

This legislation, Mr. President, seeks peace and stability for free men in a free world. It seeks them by economic rather than by military means. It proposes to help our friends to help themselves in the pursuit of sound and successful liberty in the democratic pattern. The quest can mean as much to us as it does to them. It aims to preserve the victory against aggression and dictatorship which we thought we won in World War II. It strives to help stop World War III before it starts. It fights the economic chaos which would precipitate far-flung disintegration. It sustains western civilization. It means to take western Europe completely off the American dole at the end of the adventure. It recognizes the grim truth—whether we like it or not—that American self-interest, national economy, and national security are inseverably linked with these objectives. It stops if changed conditions are no longer consistent with the national interest of the United States. It faces the naked facts of life.

Within the purview of this plan are 270,000,000 people of the stock which has largely made America. . . . They are struggling, against great and ominous odds, to regain their feet. They must not be allowed to fall. The world—America emphatically included—needs them as both producers and consumers. Peace needs their healthy restoration to the continuing defense of those ideals by which free men live. This vast friendly segment of the earth must not collapse. The iron curtain must not come to the rims of the Atlantic either by aggression or by default.

Whatever we are to do, Mr. President, let it be done without undue delay. Whatever our answer is to be, let it be made as swiftly as prudence will permit. The exposed frontiers of hazard move almost hourly to the west. Time is of the essence in this battle for peace, even as it is in the battles of a war. Nine months ago Czechoslovakia wanted to join western Europe in this great enterprise for stability and peace. Remember that. Today Czechoslovakia joins only such enterprise as Moscow may direct.

There is only one voice left in the world, Mr. President, which is competent to hearten the determination of the other nations and other peoples in western Europe to survive in their own choice of their own way of life. It is our voice. It is in part the Senate's voice. Surely we can all agree, whatever our shades of opinion, that the hour has struck for this voice to speak as soon as possible. I pray it speaks for weal and not for woe.

The committee has rewritten the bill to consolidate the wisdom shed upon the problem from many sources. It is the final product of 8 months of more intensive study by more devoted minds than I have ever known to concentrate upon any one objective in all my 20 years in Congress. It has its foes—some of whom compliment it by their transparent hatreds. But it has its friends—countless, prayerful friends not only at the hearthstones of America, but under many other flags. It is a plan for peace, stability, and freedom. As such, it involves the clear self-interest of the United States. It can be the turning point in history for 100 years to come.

If it fails, we have done our final best. If it succeeds, our children and our children's children will call us blessed. May God grant His benediction upon the ultimate event.

# III

## A GREAT AMERICAN

The editors of *Time* magazine assessed Vandenberg's role in the Senate and traced his journey from the isolationist camp of the 1930's to his bipartisan, internationalist leadership of the 1940's. The editorial excerpt which follows was written a week after Vandenberg's death.  □  "The Congress—A Great American." New York: *Time* , Volume 57, Number 18, April 30, 1951, pp. 27–28. Reprinted by permission from *Time* The Weekly Newsmagazine; copyright Time Inc. © 1951.

It was Jan. 10, 1945. A big, white-haired man with an owlish look rose at his desk in the U.S. Senate and began to read from the manuscript before him. His resonant voice rolled across the quiet chamber: "Each of us can only speak according to his little lights — and pray for a composite wisdom that shall lead us to high, safe ground." So Arthur Hendrick Vandenberg, of Michigan, swung into a 39-minute oration which galvanized the Senate.

U.S. security, he argued, could be won only by continuing to act in concert with other nations. "I do not believe that any nation hereafter can immunize itself by its own exclusive action," he said. "Our oceans have ceased to be moats." He wanted the U.S. to go forward into a new internationalism — the only road, as he saw it, to world peace. . . .

. . . It was one of the dramatic moments of congressional history. For 20 years, Arthur Vandenberg had been a Hamiltonian nationalist (he had written three books on his hero). In the years before World War II, his nationalism had led him into isolationism. On that day in January, he stood at a crossroads.

The speech in which he announced his change of mind transcended party politics, laid the groundwork for bipartisanship in foreign policy ("unpartisanship" he preferred to call it), and lifted Congressmen up to a new faith. Senator Vandenberg was not the single author of bipartisanship, but he was its acknowledged leader. As such, and as the man who knew precisely what measures would get Senate approval, and as a man who could drive those measures through, Arthur Vandenberg was the most important U.S. foreign-policy leader in Congress for the crucial years 1945-49.

. . . At 44, he announced himself a candidate for the U.S. Senate against an able Democrat, the incumbent Woodbridge N. Ferris. The able Democrat died. The governor appointed Vandenberg to fill out the term. He was subsequently elected in 1928, re-elected in 1934, 1940 and 1946.

. . . He was energetic, grandiloquent, an inveterate smoker of the denicotinized cigars which were to become almost a trademark. He was thoroughly aware of his senatorial position. His sharp-eyed critics in the press gallery dubbed him "the pouter pigeon with the kewpie smile." In domestic politics, he voted against the more radical measures of the New Deal, but voted for relief, Social Security, the New Deal housing program. He was the father of the Federal Deposit Insurance Act.

In foreign policy, in the years before World War II, he generally closed his own eyes and tried to close the eyes of the nation to any affairs overseas. Four weeks after Germany invaded Poland, he said: "This so-called war is nothing but about 25 people and propaganda." He voted against the draft act and its extension, against Lend-Lease, against the repeal of the Neutrality Act.

. . . [On] that day in January 1945, an ordinary man became an extraordinary man, applauded for his eloquence, admired for his courage. Arthur Vandenberg's "little light" became, indeed, a considerable beacon.

He spoke at a moment when the near-victorious alliance of the United Nations was beginning to show its first cracks. Vandenberg, like others at that moment, still failed to detect where the real stress lay. He interpreted Russia's hungry reaching out for neighboring states as merely an effort to shield herself in the future from a sometime rearmed Germany and Japan. He misread, or failed to read the axioms of Lenin. But in broadest terms, he was right.

Franklin Roosevelt, grateful for Vandenberg's Senate speech, appointed him a delegate to the United Nations founding convention in San Francisco. Vandenberg went to San Francisco with the firm intention of getting the need for an international bill of rights written into the U.N. Charter, and liberalizing the restrictive Dumbarton Oaks draft (particularly on the rights of neighboring nations to join in pacts of mutual defense). He won his points.

. . . Vandenberg became a delegate to U.N. General Assemblies. He accompanied his old Senate friend, James Byrnes, then Secretary of

State, to Europe. By then Vandenberg had begun to discover the true nature of Communism. In Paris, after sitting across from the Russians for 213 days, he persuaded himself and helped persuade Byrnes of the validity of a new policy of "patience and firmness." He was no Republican handmaiden of Administration policy. He was sharply critical of the Administration's vacillating China policy. Vandenberg went along with the Administration only on those proposals on which he had been consulted in advance and had had a chance to approve or modify.

It was in the Senate, his natural habitat, that he was most effective. When the Republicans captured Congress in 1946, Vandenberg became chairman of the Foreign Relations Committee. In the two years in which he guided it, his committee considered 31 bills and resolutions, passed every one unanimously. Among them were the Truman Doctrine, the "Rio Treaty," the European Recovery Program. It was largely through Vandenberg's skill as a legislator that the massive funds for ERP were successfully pushed through Congress.

. . . In those two years, the U.S. had taken some of the most momentous steps in its history. Vandenberg not only guided the steps with his eloquent, sometimes florid, always earnest, espousal of U.S. internationalism; he made them possible. At a time when no Democrat stepped forward to take leadership of the nation's foreign-policy program, Vandenberg assumed the burden. He rode herd on the balkiest members of his own party, hammered patchwork Administration proposals into workable legislation. He was talked about for the 1948 Republican presidential nomination, but would do nothing whatever to further his own chances. Sitting at night in his Wardman Park Hotel suite, he pecked out on his old typewriter the speeches that determined the course of many a foreign-policy debate. With the Vandenberg Resolution, he laid the basis for the structure which was to become, a few years later, the North Atlantic Treaty Organization.

But by then Vandenberg was a sick man, racked by intermittent headaches. In July 1949, he was to make the last important speech of his career. He appealed in the Senate for support of the North Atlantic Treaty. It was the reaffirmation, once more, of Arthur Vandenberg's belief in the nation's new role in the world. "Once upon a time we were a comfortable, isolated land," he said. "Now we are unavoidably the leader and the reliance of free men throughout this free world. We cannot escape from our prestige nor from its hazard." Vandenberg prayed that the world would not misinterpret U.S. motives. The U.S., he said, only wanted peace—but it must be "peace with righteousness."

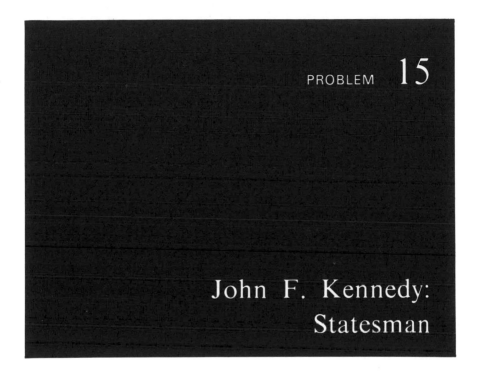

PROBLEM 15

# John F. Kennedy:
# Statesman

Perhaps no other man in politics has touched the hearts and challenged the minds of so many young people as John Fitzgerald Kennedy. His grave in Arlington Cemetery attracts more tourists than any other place in the national capital. Thousands of books and articles have been written about him and his family. For young Americans he has won places beside Washington as a hero and next to Lincoln as a martyr.

Kennedy's influence was felt by the entire world, yet his skills were those of men whose influence was more limited. As did other great decision makers, he had within him a touch of the agitator, a bit of the theorist, and a large share of the political manipulator. He could turn a phrase as skillfully as Samuel Adams, talk about the nature of politics as well as John Calhoun, and pull strings as masterfully as Mark Hanna. Kennedy used these skills to create a distinctive political style which carried his leadership beyond his position as President.

Kennedy was born in 1917 in Brookline, Massachusetts. He was the grandson of John F. "Honey Fitz" Fitzgerald, mayor of Boston when the Irish were beginning to gain control of politics in that city, and the son of Joseph P. Kennedy, financier and one-time ambassador to the Court

154

of St. James's. John Kennedy was accustomed to position and privilege from birth. After graduating from Harvard, he served with great distinction in the United States Navy during World War II. With the help of his family's wealth as well as the political connections and charm of the entire clan, he climbed the political ladder from the House of Representatives to the Senate to the presidency. He was assassinated after almost three years as the Chief Executive.

In the years since his death, many of the plans he formulated have been developed and put into effect by his vice-presidential choice, Lyndon B. Johnson. Kennedy's words, his deeds, and his spirit are now preserved for the nation in the Kennedy Library in Boston.

As you read, think about the following questions:

**1**    What were Kennedy's major personal attributes? How were they useful in politics? How were they useful to Kennedy as a leader?

**2**    What were Kennedy's skills as a politician? as a leader?

**3**    What were Kennedy's goals? How did he hope to reach them? How many could be reached through legislation? Which ones required a different approach?

## KENNEDY'S STYLE OF LEADERSHIP

Richard H. Rovere, a skilled Washington reporter who has written extensively about American politics, wrote the following article shortly after President Kennedy was assassinated.  ☐  Richard H. Rovere, "Letter from Washington." *The New Yorker,* November 30, 1963, pp. 51–53. Reprinted by permission; copyright © 1963 The New Yorker Magazine, Inc.

When we think of him, he is without a hat, standing in the wind and the weather. He was impatient of topcoats and hats, preferring to be exposed, and he was young enough and tough enough to confront and to enjoy the cold and the wind of these times, whether the winds of nature or the winds of political circumstance and national danger. He died of exposure, but in a way that he would have settled for—in the line of duty, and with his friends and enemies all around, supporting him and shooting at him. It can be said of him, as of few men in a like position, that he did not fear the weather, and did not trim his sails, but instead challenged the wind itself, to improve its direction and to cause it to blow more softly and more kindly over the world and its people. . . .

The familiar measures of political effectiveness, diplomatic skill, and the ability to preserve national unity are quite inadequate for appraising the Republic's loss. As a chief magistrate, performing the functions required of him by his oath, John Kennedy was, as they say in the Senate, able and distinguished. He was also subtle, imaginative, daring, and — to use a word he liked — prudent. He had, then, most of the qualities that are called for in a statesman if the statesman is to do the single most important thing required of him, which is, specifically, to keep the ship of state from being blown out of the water — to keep everything from going to hell and gone. Lincoln and Roosevelt were great because they performed prodigies of rescue and salvage, because they kept the worst from happening. Kennedy had two superb moments as a statesman. In the first, during the Cuban crisis in October of last year [1962], he did what was essentially a job of high-class fire prevention. In the second, when he proclaimed a state of "moral crisis" in June of this year, he did something a bit more creative. He used words to shame his countrymen, to make them look at the squalor about them. To be sure, it took only normal vision to see that there was a "moral crisis" in the United States in the summer of 1963. It was no less apparent than the earlier "missile crisis." What Kennedy undertook was a rescue job, begun close to the point of despair.

Again, this is what a statesman does, or what a good statesman does. Many statesmen do less. The opportunity to do more is rarely given to anyone — and, as often as not, when it is given, and grasped, disaster ensues, and the fire department must be called. In doing the things that simply had to be done, Kennedy had, as a rule, uncommon skill and finesse and very sharp eyes. It was not, however, his primary gift for politics that created — especially in the first days but also whenever, in the days that followed, history allowed him a few easy breaths and a bit of time for speculation — the air of excitement and immense possibility that could be felt in Washington, whether or not it was felt much outside. What made for excitement was that Kennedy and those who were closest to him — those whom he had freely chosen to associate himself with — had large, bold aims and a large, expansive view of life. There was not a reformer among them, as far as anyone could tell. Pragmatism — often of the grubbiest kind — was rampant. "Facts" were often valued beyond their worth. "Ideology" was held in contempt — too much so, perhaps — and was described as a prime source of mischief in the world. But if there were no do-gooders around, and no planners, and not even, really, very much in the way of plans, there were large thoughts and large intentions and very long looks into the future. Under Kennedy, for the first time in American history, a foreign policy was being fashioned that looked several administrations ahead, several decades ahead, several adversaries ahead. The unitary, jihad [crusading] view of foreign affairs that had dominated American thinking for so long was scrapped—and without anyone's saying much about it. There was more to the world that Kennedy saw than the Cold War. The aim of his disarmament policy was not merely to relax tensions in the years in which he thought he would be responsible for American diplomacy but to de-fuse conflict in a world that can thus far only be imagined, and even now can hardly be mentioned—one in which there could be higher tensions than any the Cold War ever generated. Kennedy was never concerned with "winning" the Cold War. He saw that it wasn't going to be won or lost, and that one real danger was that unless the United States composed its differences with the Soviet Union, its power to influence events would decline in those parts of the world where the Cold War would be regarded, properly, as an irrelevancy.

There were many such enterprises, some of them less abstract and inherently more interesting. Kennedy's mind was not a philosophical tool but a critical one. He had, above all, a critical intelligence and a critical temper—these, and a curiosity as broad as Montaigne's. He was interested in and amused by and critical of everything in American life. His zest for simply watching the show was as great as H. L. Mencken's. His curiosity seemed at times not only astonishing in itself but almost frivolous, almost perverse; he would spend time (government time) talking and bothering about things in a way that somehow seemed idle and improper for a man who should have been thinking about Khrushchev, de Gaulle, and the tax bill—the typography of a newspaper, for example, and how much it offended him, and how it might be improved. This critical bent, though, was the important, stimulating thing. He could not, with his sort of mind, look at American life and think that everything would be jim-dandy if we just had medicare and stepped up production in our engineer factories and got Negroes into nice, clean motels. As he was the first Abolitionist President (in the sense that he was the first to take office with the conviction, not passionate but sturdy, that no form of segregation or discrimination was morally defensible), so he was the first modern President who gave one a sense of caring—and of believing that a President ought to care—about the whole quality and tone of American life. (Theodore Roosevelt and Woodrow Wilson had some of this, but not so much. The others either have not cared or have been hobbyists of a sort—like Franklin Roosevelt, with his dabbling in architecture.) Kennedy's concern with motels was not only with whether Negroes should get into them but with the *idea* of motels—with their function, with the way they looked, with the strange names they bore, and with what they revealed about us. His concern with urban rot and the urban sprawl was not simply that of the criminologist or the social worker or the transit engineer but that of the man who recoils at ugliness and vulgarity and intellectual impoverishment whether or not they are associated with juvenile delinquency, unemployment, and so on. His concern with education ran far deeper than his publicly expressed concern over whether there was, quantitatively, enough of it and whether it should have federal aid and on what basis; he was interested in its character and in the direction it was taking — in whether it was any good or not.

His interests far outran his mandate; some of them, indeed, may have been unconstitutional. He proposed to have, in time, an impact on American taste. He proposed to impress upon the country — to make it, if he could, share — his own respect for excellence of various kinds. His respect for excellence was, he knew, greater than his capacity for identifying it and appreciating it. He himself did not respond much to painting or music, or even to literature — though as a rule he found his attention riveted by almost anything in print — but he looked at paintings he didn't enjoy, and listened to music he didn't much care for, because people who he thought were excellent people had told him they were excellent things, and he wished his own patronage (the picture of him alertly pursuing self-improvement) to win from others the appreciation of those things that their excellence merited. In any man but a President — and perhaps even in a President — this sort of thing might be the opposite of admirable; the father who lays down Mickey Spillane long enough to tell his bored son that every American boy should have a fine time reading "Il Penseroso" is a sinner of some kind. But Kennedy did believe — and did act upon the belief — that a President of the United States could do more than help insure domestic tranquillity, secure the blessings of liberty, and the rest. He thought that a President might help a fundamentally good society to become a good, even a brilliant, civilization. And it pleased him to think of himself as a promoter, an impresario. He was a shrewd enough observer to know that there are always a number of Americans who look in the mirror and see reflected there the President of the United States — or who make certain alterations that will enable them to see that reflection. (This didn't take much shrewdness when new trends in male and female hair styles began to develop a few years back, or when the Casals White House record began to sell — he kept checking the sales figures as though he had been cut in on the royalties — or when the mail began to come in from people who were taking up calisthenics and hiking.)

What Truman did for sports shirts, what Eisenhower did for golf, Kennedy planned — with the most deliberate kind of intent — to do for the things and the people and the institutions he thought excellent, and thus deserving. Perhaps in death he will gain more immediate success than he would have gained if he had lived on. It will hardly be fair to him, though, if it happens that way. He wished to do it by sneak plays of his own devising.

It was not Kennedy's little promotions — Casals, Robert Frost, the Mona Lisa, French cooking, Ian Fleming, Harvard College, Stravinsky, Whig history, the London *Observer* — that were stimulating but, rather, the idea that he might do something to advance American civilization. And if this idea has, as it must have, a fatuous sound, that was somehow part of it; it was moving and exciting in its fatuousness. What was also moving, and not at all fatuous, was the admiration for excellence that led Kennedy to surround himself, as much as he could, with the best people our present civilization has to offer, and to give them, as much as he could, their heads. If he had to rely on the judgment of others for the identification of excellence in the arts and the sciences, his instinct for excellence in people was, if not unerring, fine — itself excellent. (It was pretty close to unerring if one counts only those with whom he surrounded himself in government, and leaves out of account some of those he had about him at such times as he wearied of cerebration and high policy.) He had simply enormous confidence in broad, general, generalizing human intelligence. Mere expertise seemed to bother him, possibly because he had little of it himself, in anything. He was an educated man, not a trained one. At any rate, he felt that any adequately educated man with a really good head on his shoulders could get on top of just about any problem that a President was likely to face. When he found a brilliant young man like Theodore Sorenson, he commissioned him to function as an expert on anything that came along. McGeorge Bundy became his principal adviser on foreign policy with qualifications that no other recent President would have given two cents for. Bundy had worked on a couple of books about Henry Stimson and Dean Acheson, but his experience in the field of his responsibilities was almost nonexistent; he had done a good job of pulling things together on the Harvard faculty, and Kennedy took him on to pull things together in the world. Adam Yarmolinsky, a lawyer who had served a hitch as an editor in a publishing house, was put in the Pentagon to see if mere reason and common sense could be applied to its staggering problems of organization and finance. The impact he has had on the military establishment — as one of the chief Whiz Kids, the computerized intellectual task force that so enrages Senator [John L.] McClellan—has probably been as great as that of most civilian secretaries or most members of the Joint Chiefs of Staff. Perhaps the most striking case of this kind, though surely the least known, is that of Richard N. Goodwin, a lawyer who hadn't turned thirty when Kennedy engaged him, and who has spent the last three years jumping all over the government.... The most revealing part of...[Goodwin's] story is that whatever his title happened to be at the moment, his relationship to John F. Kennedy was the same and his functions were pretty much the same. He wrote speeches on everything, he continued to be an important expert on Latin America, and he was an adviser on the arts long before it was decided to give him such a title. He decided one day early in 1961 that this country should really do something about saving the Nile monuments, and he worked out a plan, which was followed. More recently, he addressed himself to a scheme for getting around the Congressional resistance to foreign aid by finding congenial projects in this field that state governments could undertake. He kicked this off last year by persuading the State of California to undertake a program of aid to Chile, on goodness knows what theory—perhaps just that Chile is also long and narrow and washed by the Pacific.

It is unlikely that any other President in our time will operate in such a fashion. But Kennedy's reliance on general excellence received one great vindication, more or less in reverse. Only once, on a really crucial matter, did he close his ears to his generalists and rely wholly on expertise. That was, of course, the Bay of Pigs [April 1961], when the people who knew the most were shown to know the least, and those who used nothing much more than the brains God gave them were proved mostly right. Among the generalists he stood first, for he was the one who had felt the gravest skepticism. He cursed himself for suppressing it. No mistake of a similar nature or of comparable magnitude was subsequently made. The things he can now be said to have accomplished are few in number, but he was prepared—indeed, he found the prospect far from dismaying—to go through two terms and face just such a judgment on his accomplishments. Once, early in 1962, his artist friend William Walton brought to the President's office a scale model of the projected remodelling of Lafayette Square. The President spent an inordinate amount of time talking about it and moving little pieces around. Walton was embarrassed. He apologized for detaining the President so long over a matter that was so far from earth-shaking—so far, even, from nation-shaking. "No, let's stay with it," the President said. "Hell, this may be the only thing I'll ever really get done." Kennedy wished very much to be known and written about as a great President, and he took a chance on having history judge him not for the things he actually completed in his time but for the things he set in motion, the energies he released, the people and ideas he encouraged, the style he brought to the Presidency. Even now it is possible to say that he set a great deal in motion, that he organized a generation of public servants who will be serving Presidents (and perhaps being Presidents) into the next century, that he made thinking respectable in Washington, and that he brought to the Presidency a genuinely distinctive style, which is bound, in time, to be emulated.

PB-33146
5-08

6 7 8 9 10 11 12 13 14 15 16 17 18 19 20 21 22 23 24 25  SH  74 73 72 71 70 69